Th[illegible] of Fl[illegible]ubs

Stanley B. Whitehead D.Sc.

Illustrated by Joan Lupton

FREDERICK WARNE

Published by Frederick Warne (Publishers) Ltd, London, 1984

Cover picture, *Chaenomeles* 'Nicoline',
supplied by Harry Smith Horticultural
Photographic Collection

Material in this book, now fully revised and updated, originally formed part of *The Observer's Book of Flowering Trees and Shrubs*, by the same author.

ISBN Limp 0 7232 3167 2
ISBN Cased 0 7232 3194 X

Printed and bound in Great Britain by William Clowes Limited,
Beccles and London

Contents

Introduction

Shrubs in the Modern Garden

Botanically, shrubs are perennial plants with several separate and persistent woody stems growing from or near their base. Trees differ in that they bear their top growth branching from a single stem or trunk, though this is sometimes so short that the plant appears shrub-like. Such plants provide the permanent ornamental furnishings of the modern garden; initially costly, but economically easy to care for and maintain.

The important points that should govern their choice are their size in height and breadth when mature; their form and habit of growth; their hardiness; their fitness for the situation and soil in which they are to grow. In small gardens shrubs may be interplanted among flowers in a bed or border, using shrubs that are not only floriferous in themselves but having good foliage to contrast with the colour provided by the herbaceous or other flowers in their season. The place of trees may be more suitably filled by taller growing shrubs, which are ideal for lawns, for the end of vistas, and as specimens growing alone. Small flowering or berrying or pleasing evergreen shrubs in containers, tubs or vases may be used on paved terraces, patios, forecourts, or in circumscribed town gardens.

Shrub Borders The real art of shrub gardening, however, lies in using these plants in a border, belt or group planned as a composite and complete unity. It is better to concentrate on a few of the best genera and species of shrubs than to attempt to embrace them all. One way is to group like species and varieties together. For example, the grouping of *Berberis*, *Cistus*, *Escallonia*, *Genista*. *Hebe*, *Helianthemum*, *Hydrangea*, *Potentilla*, and *Rosa*, makes glorious seasonal displays.

In planning the shrubbery proper, however, over-crowding is an evil to avoid. Each individual plant should have sufficient room to develop naturally and to reach a mature size. It can then display its true quality.

Modern gardens are the out-door living rooms of the home. The nearer to the buildings that shrubs are planted, the more important it is to use those of apt size and shape; correctly chosen, shrubs can help 'fit' a house into its setting as few other plants can.

The design of a shrub garden must necessarily be subordinate to the space available. It should, however, be planned on informal, natural lines. The sweeping curve, the round or the irregularly elliptical edge to borders or beds is more fitting to the natural habit of ornamental shrubs than is the straight line, square or rectangle. There should be some irregularity in the placing of shrubs, and a complete avoidance of anything approaching regimentation.

In shrub gardening, the tree should be considered subordinate to the shrub. The trees which fit in best are those which cast only light shade, and which are of a stature suitable for the garden. A sensible rule-of-thumb is to plant no tree that has a height greater than one-third that of the greatest dimension of the garden.

Soils

Before choosing the shrubs we should like to grow, some consideration should be given to the soil and the situation in which they are to be planted.

The Nature of Soils The soil is the medium in which the shrub anchors itself by means of its roots and the source of various plant foods or nutrients, which consist of a range of mineral salts dissolved in the water which is present in all soils. The plant absorbs them through fine hair-like rootlets. Garden soils are made up of five components: (1) the inorganic mineral fraction; (2) the organic fraction; (3) air; (4) water; (5) soil life.The mineral matter consists of particles fragmented by weathering and other natural forces from various kinds of rock. The finest particles are microscopic, lying so closely together as to adhere easily, and are termed clay. The coarser particles consist of sands, gravel and stones. Between the finest sand and coarsest clay come intermediate particles known as silt.

The kind and proportion of particles in a soil determine its texture. A soil containing more than 15% clay is apt to be sticky, to hold water and to be heavy to work. Soils containing much sand, gravel or stones drain freely, can be cultivated easily and are called light. Silt soils are of an intermediate texture without the stickiness of clay. Since fine particles are more easily decomposed than coarse ones, clay soils are potentially richer in soluble plant foods than sandy ones.

The organic fraction of a soil consists of the decaying remains of plants and animals which are broken down to a substance known as humus and soluble nutrients for plants. The addition of humus-forming organic matter to the inert mineral earth creates a living soil.

Humus is the state of organic matter in the soil when it reaches the last stages of decomposition; amorphous, brown to black in colour, and containing a weak cement, binding soil particles together, to make all soils more granular or crumbed. It is colloidal or glue-like, absorbing moisture and becomes a reservoir for soluble plant food. Humus lightens the texture of clay while increasing the ability of sands to hold moisture.

Air and water occupy the spaces between the particles of the soil. Both are essential to the biochemistry of soil and plant nutrition. They should, however, be present in good balance. Too much water and too little air means a cold wet soil in which plant roots may rot.

The soil life is floral and faunal. There are tiny algae, lichens and fungi living in the soil, living out their life cycles, and in decay adding to its humus. Fungi break down added organic matter and may help in the feeding of plants. The most important soil organisms, however, are the bacteria of which it is estimated more than 2,000,000,000 may be found in a salt-spoonful of soil.

Together with fungi, bacteria feed on organic remains in the soil and are responsible for their decomposition. There are bacteria which fix nitrogen from the air, bacteria which convert complex nitrogenous compounds into nitrates that plants can use, and bacteria which free other plant foods from organic material and from the mineral particles of the soil.

Other soil organisms include beneficial earth-worms and nematodes which tunnel the soil to improve its aeration and drainage and to mix mineral and organic fractions together. The soil may also be frequented by various fungi, eel-worms, insects and animals parasitic on other organisms or plants. Under good cultivation, however, such parasites can be controlled.

As a result of the inter-activity between these five constituents the soil water becomes a dilute solution of the soluble salts available, on which plant roots feed.

Just how well plants can exploit the soil solution depends partly upon its acid-alkaline balance, which governs the kind and quantity of nutrients available to them. In garden soils, this balance is usually governed by the presence or absence of lime, and is measured by what is called *p*H scale.

On the *p*H scale *p*H 7 indicates a neutral solution. Ratings lower than 7 indicate acidity; ratings higher than 7 indicate alkalinity. The *p*H rating of any soil is an indication of its hydrogen-ion concentration. This can be detected electrically by the use of a simple soil *p*H meter, or colormetrically by the use of sensitive dye solutions embodied in a gardener's soil testing outfit; both are available at garden centres and shops.

Most garden plants grow best in acid to slightly acid soils of *p*H 5·5 to 6·5, and ornamental shrubs tolerate and like a soil *p*H of 5 to 6·5. Acidity is corrected by adding lime, the amount depending upon the degree of acidity to be corrected and the kind of lime used. Alkalinity is more difficult to correct, requiring the use of sulphur, aluminium and ferrous sulphates, peat, organic manures, and acid fertilizers.

In considering soils suitable for ornamental shrubs a clear distinction must be drawn between the soils that contain lime and those that are lime-free. The presence of lime, even in an acid soil, is not tolerated by certain species, particularly those of the Ericaceae, itemed under *Peat Soils* later in this chapter.

Clay Soils The characteristics of clay soils are tenacity, plasticity when wet, heaviness to cultivate, and tendency to lie wet and cold. Most clay soils, unless the clay is of the type known as marl, are also acid. To improve them, clay soils require horticultural gypsum at 272–544 gr per sq m (8–16 oz per sq yd) and liberal dressings of humus-forming organic material, chiefly rotted manure, compost, peat, leafmould, spent hops, chopped straw or bracken, forked into the top-soil when the soil is roughly dug in the autumn or early winter. If strongly acid, lime may follow in the winter, using ground limestone at 272–408 gr per sq m (8–12 oz per sq yd).

The addition of coarse sand, coke breeze, gravel, etc, is helpful to improve texture, but can only be attempted in a small way. What is more important is to see that the drainage is good. With good drainage and humus-enrichment, most ornamental shrubs can be grown on clay soils.

Sandy Soils have an openness of texture, free drainage, a quick response to temperature changes and a tendency to dry out. Such soils lose their soluble elements rapidly in drainage and so tend to be of poor fertility. They are, however, light and easy to work. Their primary need is organic matter—animal manures, shoddy, peat, compost, spent hops, leafmould, etc—forked into the top spit in winter and applied as mulching in summer. If easily obtainable, a tonne or two of clay per 25 sq m, (1 rod), spread roughly on the surface to weather in during winter, greatly increases moisture-holding for many years. Organic fertilizers are most helpful in building up fertility. Acid sands are best amended by the addition of ground chalk, since this material absorbs a little moisture.

As the moisture-holding capacity and the fertility of the soil are increased, a wide range of ornamental plants can be grown.

Calcareous Soils overlie chalk, limestone or marl. They contain carbonate of lime in abundance, and this makes them alkaline. To grow shrubs well, it is necessary to neutralize this alkalinity. The first essential is good drainage so that soluble lime salts are leached (washed out). Any hard or solid sub-soil rock or pan should be broken by pick or mattock. The tendency is for the top soil to lose lime to the subsoil, and it should not be brought back again.

The second need is to dress liberally with organic matter. Animal manures, compost, peat, shoddy, leafmould, sewage and green material are all useful. Acid-reacting fertilizers such as dried blood, and the sulphates of ammonia, iron, magnesium and potash can be used with advantage.

Excessive alkalinity tends to deny iron to plants and a common symptom of iron starvation in plants growing on calcareous soils is the paling of the foliage known as chlorosis.

Other nutrients may also be unavailable, and growth is thereby stunted. The modern counter is to feed plants with chelated or sequestered compounds of iron, etc (Sequestrenes) periodically.

Given adequate organic manuring, the range of shrubs which can be grown on chalk, limestone and the lighter marl soils is quite extensive.

Peat Soils are usually found on moorlands, on heaths overlying poor sand or stony soil, and in the Fens. Such soils are moisture-retentive, inclined to be deficient in potash, and are not at first highly fertile. Exposure of the peat to the air and weather aids its further decomposition; a process which can be fostered by drainage, where the peat soil is a wet one, by the addition of animal manures, or compost, and fertilizers, and if desirable by liming.

In shrub-growing, however, a peaty soil is ideal for the calcifuge plants which hate lime. These include some of the most beautiful genera in cultivation, such as:

Calluna species
Camellia species
Cassiope species
Daboecia species
Enkianthus species
Erica species
Gaultheria species
Kalmia species
Pernettya species
Pieris species
Styrax species
Vaccinium species
Zenobia species

With cultivation and the addition of lime, peat soils may also be planted with many other shrubs to vary the planting scheme.

Silt Soils Silt particles are finer than sand, yet coarser than clay, and soils rich in silt are often difficult since they neither drain freely nor have the stickiness of clay. They are apt to become compacted and inert in cultivation, and do not react to lime in the same way that clay does. The chief need of silt soils in shrub-growing is organic matter. Once this is assured, silt soils can be as productive as any other.

Their precise treatment, however, depends upon whether the texture is coarse or fine. A coarse silt soil will also contain sand, and is best cultivated on the lines suggested for a sandy soil. A fine, heavy silt soil is usually admixed with clay and may be treated and amended as a clay soil. The same criterion can be applied in deciding on the most suitable shrubs to plant.

Loamy Soils consist of various proportions of mineral particles, such as sands, silt and clay, and have a humus-forming organic matter content; they are workable and potentially fertile. Such soils are often termed heavy, medium, or light according to the mineral balance. A balance of 50 to 70% fine and coarse sand, 10 to 20% silt, and 20 to 30% clay gives the finest loams.

Garden loam is made by stacking pasture turf, cut 10–15 cm (4–6 in) thick, to decompose for at least a year, and then riddling it to provide crumbly, friable soil.

Situations

Shrubs that are native to foreign countries can only thrive in our gardens where climatic conditions are broadly similar to those of their native habitat. Latitude, altitude and geographical situation must be taken into account when choosing shrubs. Geographical position, whether coastal or inland, in the damper west or the drier east, whether facing north, south, east or west, will have a bearing in determining which shrubs will thrive and which ones will not.

Apart from the general climate, each garden has a local climate, according to the lie of the land and its relation to its surroundings. Such matters as shade and sun, nearness to towns or industrial areas, exposure to wind and frost and the actual terrain within the garden must influence the choice of plants for specific locations.

Frost-susceptible Situations Severe winter frosts may cause plant losses almost anywhere in Britain, but the greatest damage is done by untimely frosts in spring when the plants are freshly coming into growth.

Cold air, being heavier than warm, collects at and near ground level and flows over the contours of the ground to the lowest parts. Consequently, gardens in valleys, on low-lying ground, or in pockets are most likely to sustain spring frost damage. Here it is wise to plant the hardiest of shrubs and, to ensure a good show, to plant only species and varieties which flower when the danger of frost is past.

Windy Situations Wind may sometimes be formidable for its mechanical force but is far more so for its climatic effect. Wind accentuates the effect of the climatic conditions in which it blows. Winds coinciding with spring frost increase the cold's deadliness. The art of minimizing the effect of wind lies in breaking its force up into minor turbulences. A trellis or openwork fence or boundary planting of suitable shrubs or trees is more effective than an impenetrable obstruction.

No shrubs are draught-proof, but for exposed situations, the following are useful as a first line of defence against winds:

Cotoneaster simonsii
Hippophae rhamnoides
Ilex aquifolium
Ligustrum ovalifolium
Lonicera yunnanensis
Olearia × *haastii*
Prunus cerasifera
Prunus spinosa
Sambucus nigra
Tamarix gallica
Ulex europaeus

For gardens on the coast where winds are often laden with salt spray, the following are more suitable:

Escallonia macrantha and vars
Euonymus species
Hippophae rhamnoides
Senecio rotundifolius
Tamarix tetrandra

Shady Situations All green plants are dependent on light for their nutrition and energy but vary in the amount of light they need or can tolerate. Broadly it may be said that the plants which do best in full sun are those with softish leaves well equipped with pores (stomata) and an internal structure through which carbon dioxide gas diffuses quickly. Plants which can tolerate and grow in shade are those with rather tough, darkish leaf structures that diffuses CO_2 slowly.

Dry Situations Plants which can stoutly resist both the limiting effects of a parched dry soil and an exposed site such as on a terrace, bank or wall, are chiefly to be sought among the grey or narrow-leaved shrubs such as:

Cistus species
Cotoneaster microphylla
Cytisus species
Genista species
Helianthemum species
Lavandula species
Rosmarinus officinalis
Santolina species
Spartium junceum
Tamarix species
Ulex europaeus

Wet Situations No shrubs will thrive in water-logged conditions where the water is stagnant, but the following can be planted with confidence beside water and in wet situations from which the water does drain, even if only slowly:

Aronia species
Cornus species
Kalmia species
Skimmia species
Symphoricarpos species
Vaccinium species

Planting

Good planting ensures the rapid recovery of the shrub from the shock of moving, and preserves its future good shape and symmetry. Most garden soils can be best be prepared by bastard trenching: a thorough turning over of the top spit and a breaking up of the second spit or subsoil where it lies.

Soil Treatment before Planting Thoroughly rotted organic matter, manure or compost, or moist peat, should be worked into the top soil. Artificial fertilizers are not desirable. Bone meal, hoof and horn meal are helpful on most soils. On light hungry soils, seaweed meal will aid rooting action and strengthen disease resistance.

Planting Time Deciduous shrubs and trees may be planted out in mild weather, when the soil is workable, from late October to early April. Evergreen shrubs should be moved either in early autumn, from September to November, or from mid-March to May.

Some shrubs do not move well and are consequently usually grown in pots and containers and can be planted at almost any time of the year except during weather extremes. Trees and shrubs received from the nursery during a period of frost or when the soil is too waterlogged for planting are best placed in a shallow trench at a slanting angle of 45°, their roots heaped over with soil until *favourable* planting conditions return.

Stock for Planting Shrubs naturally transplant most easily when young, and in choosing stock for planting, preference is best given to juvenile plants of sturdy growth, well furnished with fibrous roots.

Planting Technique The planting hole should be dug at least one-third again as wide as the spread of the roots. If the sub-soil has not been broken up previously, this should be done and the soil re-firmed.

Most shrubs are planted to the same soil level as previously grown. Coarse woody roots can be pruned. Other roots can be spaced evenly, and each root must be firmly embraced by the loamy compost, and soil should be worked into the interstices of the root system with the hands before finally topping to soil level and watering well. A mulch of organic litter is then spread over the rooting area, leaving the soil around the base of the plant clear.

Plants moved with roots in a ball of soil may be soaked in water prior to planting.

Support against wind-rocking for large shrubs in exposed positions is secured by stakes driven into the soil before filling the planting hole. The ties should be loose enough to allow for growth expansion of the stems.

Propagation of Shrubs from Seeds

Shrubs raised from seeds usually develop into healthy, longlived plants. They do, however, take rather a long time growing to flowering age and good size. Only general principles can be given here, while special indications for species requiring different techniques are given in the main text of the book. The seeds should be fully ripe, especially when home-saved. The normal time to sow is in the late winter or spring months. Seed capsules, berries, etc, should be collected when ripe and stored under cool, dry conditions until required. Seed berries or fruits are best layered between layers of damp sand in boxes, and the seeds later rubbed out from the pulp when sowing time arrives.

To germinate well, seeds need only air, moisture and warmth. Temperatures for germination run rather higher than those necessary for the growth of the seedling and plant. Air and moisture are provided by choosing a suitable soil and sowing the seeds at the correct depth.

Broadly, seeds of shrubs native to temperate zones similar in climate to our own can be sown out of doors, preferably in prepared seed beds of free-draining sandy loam in a warm sheltered location in the garden. Seeds of tropical or sub-tropical species usually need to be sown under glass with the stimulus of artificial heat. Seeds of alpine species and those native to cold climates may need to be subjected to the actions of frost and snow before geminating successfully.

To have the process of germination under careful watch and control, the seeds may be sown in boxes, pots or pans, subsequently stood in propagating cases, greenhouses or cold frames according to the conditions required. The soil compost should be a modern soilless compost or the John Innes Seeds Compost consisting of:

3 parts by bulk of sterilized loam
2 parts by bulk of sedge or moss peat
1 part by bulk of coarse sand or perlite plus
42 gr ($1\frac{1}{2}$ oz) of superphosphate and 21 gr ($\frac{3}{4}$ oz) of ground chalk or ground limestone per bushel (36 litres) of mixed compost.

For lime-hating species, such as *Erica* and *Rhododendron*, the chalk or limestone should be omitted.

The depth at which to sow seeds is roughly twice their diameter. Germination time varies. In some species it may take several months. Where there is some risk of the seeds drying out before they germinate it is helpful to cover the surface of the compost with finely chopped moist sphagnum moss or perlite and sow the seeds in this.

After germination, seedlings may grow rapidly. Those already out of doors should be allowed to complete a season of growth before being moved. Those in seed containers may be carefully transplanted to a richer soil compost in pots when they have made their first true leaves, and later hardened off until the season is appropriate to plant them out of doors.

Vegetative Propagation

This practice enables us to reproduce plants identical with a parent, and this allows quick multiplication of a desirable specimen. The simplest method is by means of 'cuttings'—portions of the stems or shoots, or roots, or leaves.

Stem cuttings Cuttings of the stem or shoot are of three kinds according to when they are taken; 'hardwood' cuttings, 'softwood' cuttings, or half-ripe cuttings with a 'heel'.

Hardwood cuttings are taken in autumn. They are cut cleanly from firm, healthy lateral shoots of the current season's growth, with four to six buds, cut a little below a node. The cuttings are inserted in a bed of sandy loam, shaded and sheltered, with only the top bud above ground. They root very rapidly under bell glasses or cloches, and may be left to grow for a year before being moved to permanent quarters.

Softwood cuttings consist of portions of growing greenwood lateral shoots with a terminal bud or growing point, taken in early or mid-summer when firm. The lower leaves are cut off, and the cuttings, usually about 5–20 cm (2–8 in) long, inserted in a suitable soil under close conditions. In the case of some species, cuttings root readily enough when inserted in light, well-drained soil out of doors under bell-glasses or under jam-jars. But for consistent results it is best to root softwood cuttings in a mist propagating case where transpiration can be carefully controlled and the best conditions for rooting maintained.

The cuttings are inserted and firmed in along their length, and are kept moist and close until rooted, when more ventilation is needed.

Cuttings with a heel are generally the most successful. They consist of half-ripened lateral shoots of the current year's growth detached with the base or 'heel' of the older wood at their junction with the stem, in summer. The heel should be trimmed of ragged tissue and the leaves removed from the lower end. The cuttings are then inserted in sandy soil out of doors, in partial shade, and given the protection of a bell-glass, handlight, cloche or jam-jar to prevent undue moisture loss. Such cuttings root readily inserted around the rim of a flower-pot, or in a cold frame. Heeled cuttings may also be propagated in a propagating case or frame as for softwood cuttings.

Stem cuttings vary in the time they take to root or 'strike'. Rooting can, however, be quickened by treating the cuttings beforehand with one of the root-inducing growth-regulating substances or synthetic hormones. Broadly, shrubs with hollow or pithy stems are more difficult to root from cuttings than those with solid stems.

Root cuttings A few species are easily propagated by root cuttings, chiefly those which produce suckers easily. The method entails cutting the roots into 5 cm (2 in) lengths, inserting them in moist sand or cuttings compost, about 13 mm (0·5 in) deep, with the plant end uppermost, in pots. *Rhus*, *Fatsia*, *Campsis* and *Yucca* can be propagated in this way.

Leaf Cuttings Very few shrubs are propagated by leaf cuttings. Camellias may be treated this way, however. The cuttings consists of about a 2·5 cm (1 in) section of the stem with a leaf and axillary bud on it. The stem is cleanly sliced along to reduce its thickness by about one-half, and then inserted into the soil compost with the base of the leaf stalk and axillary bud just below the surface of the compost. Such cuttings are taken in late summer or early autumn.

Layering Shrubs which do not root readily from cuttings may often be propagated by layering. To soil-layer a shrub, a low or pendent branch is chosen which will easily reach the ground about 30 cm (12 in) or so from the tip. A hole is made about 10 to 20 cm (4 to 8 in) deep to take the branch when bent.

Rooting is induced by a partial disruption of the sap flow at the lowest point of the bent shoot. If the shoot is acutely bent to form a U without cracking, this is sufficient. It can be pegged down to the bottom of the hole and covered with soil, the upright end being staked 15 cm (6 in) above ground. Other ways of checking the sap flow are: notching the underside of the shoot; making a slanting slit to cut the shoot half-way through below a bud in an upward direction towards the apex; ringing, by removing a ring of bark 1·3 cm ($\frac{1}{2}$ in) wide; or by wiring, which calls for twisting a piece of wire tightly around the stem. In each case, the prepared layer is pegged down, covered with fine soil, and kept moist with about 15 cm (6 in) of the free end of the shoot projecting. Layering is best done in spring or early summer. The layered shoot is then left until well rooted, when it can be severed from the parent plant and transplanted the following autumn, but slow rooting species may take two years.

With shrubs that have few or no branches which can be layered in the soil, air-layering can be attempted. A chosen upright shoot is split, ringed or notched at the point where rooting is desired. If split, a small pebble or piece of matchstick or wire should be inserted to keep the split open. The point of injury is then enclosed in a poultice of moist sphagnum moss wrapped in a sleeve of polythene film, taped at each end.

Rooting can be speeded up by painting the point of sap interruption with one of the root-inducing, growth-regulating substances used for cuttings.

Shrubs are also propagated by budding in summer; by grafting in spring; by the culture of meristem tissue in the laboratory; techniques that are outside the scope of this book.

The Care of Shrubs

The newly planted shrub during the first season of new growth will be preoccupied in establishing its roots, and beyond watering in dry spells, no attempts to feed or fertilize it should be made. Thereafter, the care of the shrub garden is largely a matter of pruning and manuring.

Pruning Properly arranged and well cultivated, most shrubs do best without regular pruning. Pruning is, however, often helpful in shaping young plants, and it is practical to prune shrubs of no particular beauty so far as shape is concerned but which are esteemed for their flowers. Then there are over-grown shrubs which need restriction, by pruning in winter or early spring.

How to prune Hard pruning tends to provoke strong new shoots or wood growth, light pruning to foster flowering. Good pruning should hardly show, unwanted shoots being cut either to just above a bud facing the direction new growth is desired, or at the base flush with the junction of an older branch or stem. The general habit of the species, whether upright, arching, pyramidal, bushy or sprawling, should be taken into consideration.

Cuts should be made with the sharpest of knives or secateurs, giving preference to tools which do the least damage to the bark. Large cut surfaces may be dressed with a tree antiseptic (Arbrex 805 or Mildothane) to repel fungi and decay, but not tar or thick paint.

When to prune Decaying, dead or diseased growth should be removed as soon as it is seen, and burnt. Evergreen shrubs usually need very little pruning while in healthy and pleasing growth. When it is desired to cut overgrown branches back, the work should be done in spring, giving the new growth the longest season possible to mature.

Deciduous shrubs should be pruned according to their flowering habit. They may be divided into two kinds. First, there are those shrubs which flower on shoots of the previous year, including the winter-and-spring-flowering species; these should be pruned as soon as flowering is over.

The second group of shrubs, those which flower in summer or autumn on shoots grown during the current year, should be pruned in the spring when the sap is rising, when the old wood which has flowered can be cut out severely if so desired. Suckers of shrubs, such as *Syringa* (Lilac), should be twisted off the roots in spring or killed by painting with a paraquat/diquat herbicide (Weedol).

Manuring Regular digging is undesirable, since many shrubs have fine feeding roots near the surface. It is sufficient to prick over the soil in autumn or early winter, removing weeds and debris, and then applying a mulch.

The mulch may consist of wetted and partially rotted leaves, rotted vegetable compost, peat, chopped bracken or chopped clean straw, applied evenly to cover the soil to a depth of 5–10 cm (2–4 in). Sawdust may be used, though a depth of 2·5–5 cm (1–2 in), is sufficient. In summer, the soil can be mulched with lawn mowings or any suitable organic material to hand. Pulverized wood bark is good.

The use of artificial fertilizers around shrubs needs care. On the whole, it is wise to use the organic fertilizers so far as possible if and when extra feeding is necessary.

For the shrub garden, a mixture of 2 parts by weight hoof and horn meal, 4 parts bone meal, and 2 parts powdered seaweed applied at 136 to 204 gr per sq m (4–6 oz per sq yd) every third or fourth year under the annual mulch, will be found to promote balanced and healthy growth.

Foliar Feeding Since shrubs can absorb nutrients rapidly through their leaves and green top growth, foliar feeding by spraying with a dilute solution of soluble fertilizers can be invaluable in establishing delicate young plants, in helping plants to recover quickly from attack by disease, pests or adverse weather, and in promoting healthy, vigorous balanced growth for wintering.

Glossary

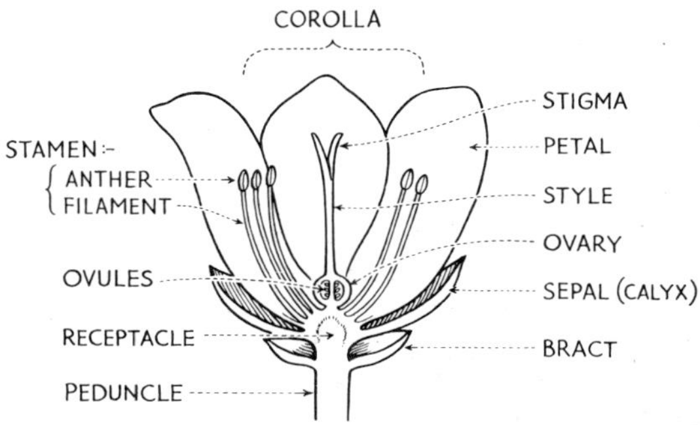

Parts of a flower

Acute ending in a point; sharp.

Alternate of leaves, arranged not opposite or whorled, but in two rows or spirally, not more than one at a node.

Anther the pollen-bearing part of the stamen.

Axil angle formed by junction of leaf or bract and stem.

Axillary growing in the axil of a leaf or bract.

Berry fleshy, several-seeded, indehiscent fruit.

Bisexual hermaphrodite, having both male and female organs in the same flower.

Blade expanded part of a leaf or petal.

Bract a modified leaf growing near the calyx of a flower.

Calcicole lime-tolerant, usually growing in soils containing free lime.

Calcifuge lime-intolerant, usually growing in acid, lime-free soils.

Calyx (pl **Calyces**) the outer whorl of floral envelopes, or sepals.

Capsule a dry fruit composed of more than one carpel.

Carpel one of the units or divisions of a pistil.

Catkin a dense, scaly-bracted spike, usually composed of unisexual, petal-less flowers.

Chlorophyll the green colouring matter of plants.

Clone group of plants with identical characteristics derived from a single individual, and propagated vegetatively.

Compound of a leaf, made up of separate leaflets; of an inflorescence, with the axis branched; of a pistil, with two or more carpels united.

Cordate heart-shaped.

Corolla the petals of a flower.

Corymb flat-topped head of stalked flowers, with outer flowers opening first.

Cyme a branching inflorescence of which the central flower opens first, with lateral branches which also have terminal flowers.

Deciduous falling-off, of plants losing their leaves in autumn.

Digitate hand-like. *See* **Palmate.**

Dioecious having the sexes on different plants.

Disk, Disc the fleshy part of the receptacle of a flower, surrounding or surmounting the pistil or ovary.

Elongate stretched out; lengthened.

Entire of leaves, having continuous margin, uncut and without teeth.

Evergreen of plants which retain their foliage green for at least a full year, remaining green throughout their dormant season.

Fastigiate having erect branches, close together.

Fertilization the process of union between male and female gametes, or reproductive cells.

Filament the stalk of the anther. *See* **Stamen.**

Florets small individual flowers, especially those in heads as of the Compositae.

Floriferous flower-bearing; producing many flowers.

Friable easily crumbled.

Fruit the seed-bearing organ, usually implies the ripe seeds and adnate structure, whether pulpy or dry.

Genus (pl **Genera**) a group of species with common structural characters.

Germination beginning of growth of a seed.

Glabrous without hairs.

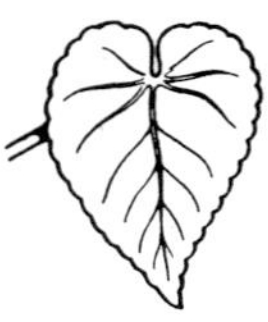

Cordate

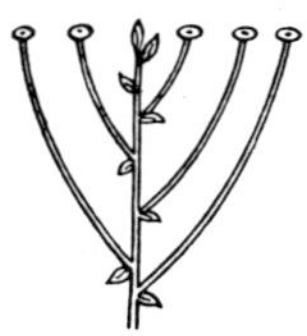

Corymb

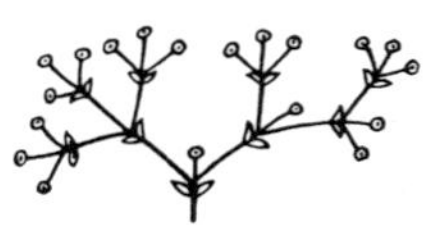

Cyme

Gland a small vesicle containing oil, resin, or other liquid, in, on or protruding from any part of a plant.

Glaucous bluish or grey, with a waxy bloom.

Herbaceous of plants in which aerial parts wither and die at the end of each growing season.

Hermaphrodite containing stamens and ovary.

Humus the state of organic matter in active decomposition in the soil.

Hybrid the offspring of the fertilization of one species by another, usually indicated by the sign ×.

Imbricated overlapping each other, like roof tiles.

Inflorescence the flowering portion and its arrangement, including stalks, bracts and flowers, on the stem.

Internode part of the stem between two nodes.

Labiate lipped.

Lanceolate lance- or spear-shaped; elliptically longer than broad, tapering to both ends.

Lateral on or at the side.

Lax loose, not compact or dense.

Leaflet secondary leaf, part of a compound leaf.

Linear long and narrow, with sides parallel or nearly so.

Lobe a part of an organ, leaf or petal, divided from the rest of it by an indentation.

Meristem a region of actively dividing cells where new tissue is formed.

Monoecious having unisexual flowers, but with both sexes on the same plant.

Node a point or joint on the stem from which one or more leaves arise.

Oblanceolate lance-shaped, but wider towards the apex or tip.

Obovate inversely ovate, with the broader end terminal.

Obtuse blunt, rounded.

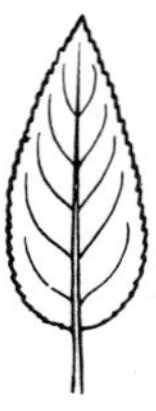

Lanceolate

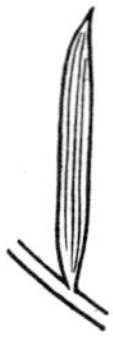

Linear

Obovate

Orbicular

Opposite of two leaves or organs arising at the same level on opposite sides of a stem.

Orbicular round or circular, length and breadth about equal.

Ovary the basal hollow part of the pistil or carpel, containing the ovules.

Ovule a body in the ovary containing the female reproductive cell which after fertilization becomes the seed.

Palmate divided like a palm or hand, usually of leaves with more than three leaflets from the same point.

Panicle a branching racemose inflorescence.

Pedicel the stalk of a single flower.

Peduncle the stalk of a flower-cluster or an inflorescence.

Perennial living for more than two years, and normally flowering each year.

Perianth the outer, non-essential floral organs, including the petals and sepals, when present.

Petiole the stalk of a leaf.

Pinnate having leaflets arranged in two rows along each side of a common stalk or axis.

Pistil the ovule- and seed-bearing organ, consisting of ovary, stigma and style.

Pistillate female, having pistils but no stamens.

Pith the soft tissue in the centre of a stem.

Pollen the spores or grains borne by the anther, containing the male element, of a flowering plant.

Pome a many-celled, fleshy fruit (e.g. apple, pear, quince).

Procumbent trailing or lying flat on the surface.

Prostrate lying closely along the surface of the ground.

Raceme a simple, elongated, unbranched inflorescence in which the flowers are borne on pedicels.

Radical of leaves arising from the root or a rhizome.

Ray-florets individual flowers in ray formation around the disc of a composite flower.

Receptacle the upper part of the stem from which the parts of the flower arise; the torus.

Oval

Palmate

Panicle

Raceme

Recurved bent backward in a curve.
Reflexed abruptly bent backward or downward.
Rib the primary vein of a leaf or other similar organ.
Rugose wrinkled.

Sagittate arrow-shaped, triangular, with basal lobes pointing downwards.
Sap the mixture of water and mineral salts rising up through a plant to fill the vacuoles in the cells.
Scape the flowering stem of a plant with all radical leaves, arising from the root.
Seed a fertilized and ripened ovule.
Self fertile a flower which can fertilize its seed by its own pollen.
Sepal one of the separate green leaves of a calyx.
Sessile stalkless.
Shrub a woody plant branching freely from the base, remaining low in form.
Simple not compound; an undivided leaf.
Species a group of individuals having the same constant and distinct characters.
Spike a simple inflorescence with the flowers sessile along an unbranched axis.
Spine a stiff, straight, sharp-pointed woody structure, usually arising from the wood of a stem.
Spreading standing out horizontally.
Spur a hollow tubular or sac-like projection from a blossom, usually secreting nectar.
Stamen the male reproductive organ of the plant, consisting of the filament and anther bearing the pollen sacs.
Sterile non-productive of seed capable of germination; of anthers not producing viable pollen.
Stigma the receptive surface or part of the pistil which receives the pollen.
Stipule a scale- or leaf-like basal appendage of a petiole, usually in pairs, and sometimes adnate.
Stoma (pl **Stomata**) a pore (pores) in the leaves and epidermis that regulates transpiration, and respiration.
Style the part of the pistil connecting the ovary and the stigma.

Sagittate

Sessile

Spatulate

Sucker a shoot rising adventitiously from the root system of a shrub or tree, often away from the base.
Syn abbreviation for synonym.

Tendril thin, modified stem, leaf or leaflet of some climbing plants; touch-sensitive, and coiling round supports.
Terminal borne at the end of a stem or branch.
Tomentose densely covered with short cottony hairs.
Tree a woody perennial plant with a single main stem (trunk) and elevated branching head.
Trifoliolate having three leaflets arising from the same point.

Umbel an inflorescence in which the flower-stalks all arise from the top of the main stem and common point, to give an umbrella-shaped head.
Undulate wavy.
Unisexual of one sex.

Var abbreviation for variety.

Whorl three or more leaves or organs of the same kind arising at the same level or node.

Stipule

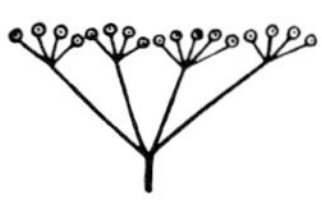

Umbel

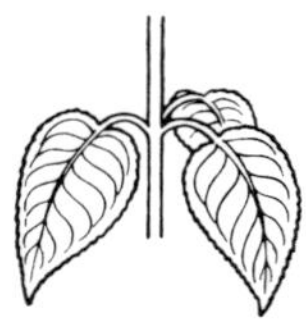

Whorl

Plant Descriptions

A note on the use of names in text and index: plant family names are printed in capitals, eg, AQUILIFOLIACEAE, the Holly family; ERICACEAE, the Heath family; ROSACEAE, the Rose family. A family embraces one genus, or more (genera), and the name of the genus is printed in italics at the head of each entry, eg, *Ilex*; *Pieris*; *Pyracantha.* A genus contains one or more species, and each species has two latin names, first the generic, followed by the specific and both given in italics, eg, *Ilex aquifolium*; *Pieris formosa*; *Pyracantha coccinea*, in the text. Species have varieties, denoted by v or var, and a third name which may be a descriptive latin epithet in italics, eg, *Ilex aquilfolium* var *pyramidalis*; *Pieris formosa* var *forrestii*; *Pyracantha coccinea* var *lalandei*; or a commemorative name which appears in quotation marks, eg, *Ilex aquifolium* 'Golden Queen'; *Pieris formosa* 'Wakehurst'; *Pyracantha coccinea* 'Orange Glow'. Varieties arising in cultivation are known as cultivars. Common names are given in roman type, where applicable, eg, Holly, Firethorn. Hybrids usually occur from the union of separate species (or varieties) of the same genus, and are marked ×. Where space allows, synonyms and common names have been included.

It is hoped that with the help of this book the reader will get to know many of his garden plants a little better, and in doing so find both more pleasure and benefit in caring for them.

Abelia
Family CAPRIFOLIACEAE

Abelia × grandiflora

A genus of attractive deciduous and evergreen shrubs, with arching stems, small, short-stalked, opposite leaves, and pink or white tubular or funnel-shaped flowers. They thrive in any well-drained loamy soil, including limy ones. Generally hardy in southern England and in mild localities, but elsewhere need shelter.

The best species are: *A. floribunda*, an evergreen from Mexico, growing 0·9–1·3 m (3–5 ft) tall, with reddish, downy stems, small, toothed, glossy green ovate leaves and rosy magenta, tubular flowers in twos or threes from June. *A. × grandiflora* is a popular hybrid, with arching shoots, up to 1·3 m (5 ft) high, ovate, shallowly toothed leaves, and pink-blush white, funnel-shaped flowers slightly scented, semi-evergreen. *A. schumannii*, from China, is deciduous with purplish downy stems, pale-green ovate leaves, and solitary, bell-shaped, rose-pink flowers from June to September; it grows to 1·2 m (4 ft) high. Stems may be killed back in hard winter, but shoot up again in spring. *A. triflora*, of the NW Himalaya, has in summer delightfully scented, white, flushed pink, flowers on branching stems up to 3 m (10 ft).

Propagate by softwood cuttings in July; by 'heeled' cuttings in September and October.

Prune out deadwood in April.

Amelanchier
Family ROSACEAE

Amelanchier oblongifolia

Easily grown and quite hardy, the Amelanchiers are a genus of deciduous shrubs or small trees, attractive for a short time in spring with hanging racemes of five-petalled white flowers but chiefly valued for their autumn colouring when the alternate, roundish, toothed leaves tint beautifully. They do well in the acid garden loams of good drainage, and like the sun.

A. laevis of North America is a graceful large shrub or tree of up to 6 m (20 ft), flowering in April. Its leaves, smooth when young, turn red in autumn. Its compatriot, *A. canadensis*, the June Berry, or Shad Bush, flowering at the same time, has young leaves that are downy, colouring magnificently in autumn. Notable also are *A. ovalis* (syn *A. vulgaris*), the Snowy Mespilus of Europe, 1·5–2 m (5–7 ft), with masses of white starry flowers in May, and black berries in autumn; *A. lamarckii*, also of Europe, bushy and spreading to 5 m (16 ft); and *A. oblongifolia*, of North America, with woolly leaves, woolly racemes of white flowers, and black edible fruits in autumn, which grows thicket-like to about 4 m (13 ft).

Propagate by fresh seeds in autumn; by softwood cuttings in July; by layering in spring; or by division in November.

Chokeberry

Aronia
Family ROSACEAE

Aronia arbutifolia

The deciduous shrubs of this North American genus of three species have threefold merit, attractive branching clusters of five-petalled white or pinkish flowers in May, colourful berried fruits, and brilliant foliage colouring in autumn. They are hardy, easily grown, and not particular as to soil.

A. arbutifolia makes a shrub of bushy habit, 150–240 cm (5–8 ft) high, with hairy shoots, alternate, ovate, finely toothed leaves of smooth dull green above, grey-haired below; white or pinkish flowers in May followed by small red berries which persist for some time, and brilliant red autumn foliage. *A. prunifolia* (syn *A. floribunda*) is similar, but flowers in looser clusters, followed by purple-black berries. The Black Chokeberry, *A. melanocarpa*, is a smaller shrub, 60–90 cm (2–3 ft) high, and lacks hairiness on its shoots, inflorescence and leaves. Its flowers are white, its berries black, and the autumn foliage turns blushing scarlet.

These shrubs are worth planting for their autumn colour alone, and their low stature makes them suitable for small gardens.

Propagate by seeds in early spring; by cuttings with a heel in late summer; or by division.

Artemisia
Family COMPOSITAE

Artemisia abrotanum

Only a few species of this large genus which includes herbaceous perennials and annual plants are shrubs. These are appreciated chiefly for their attractive, silver-greyish foliage which gives off a sweet, fragrant aroma, especially when crushed. The shrubs grow easily in any reasonably well-drained soil, but may only be truly evergreen in mild localities.

A. abrotanum, from southern Europe, has various common names (Southernwood, Lad's Love, Old Man and Old Woman), throws up erect stems to 0·9 m (3 ft) or so, is densely clad with feathery foliage of greyish green leaves, pinnately dissected to fine lobes, and is highly aromatic. The flowers are dull yellow, borne in terminal panicles, in September or October, and of no great distinction. It is more deciduous than evergreen under British conditions, and its chief garden merit is foliage contrast. *A. nutans* of the Canary Islands is silvery-white in stem and leaf, growing 0·3–0·9 m (1–3 ft), with pinnately lobed feathery foliage and pale yellow flowers in crowded leafy panicles in August.

Propagate by cuttings with a heel in July and August.

Spotted Laurel

Aucuba
Family CORNACEAE

Aucuba japonica

The species most representative of this genus and most commonly grown is *A. japonica*, a Japanese evergreen shrub 2–3 m (6·5–10 ft) tall and with as wide a spread, of rounded, bushy habit. Its large, long oval leaves are leathery glossy on both sides, and, on female plants, spotted with yellow, and resembling the Laurel. The flowers appear in March or April, small, with four purplish petals in erect terminal panicles, and are unisexual; the male with stamens, the female without. On the female, the pollinated flowers are followed by clusters of bright red oval berries. This shrub will grow under trees and in heavy shade. Since the species is dioecious, to be sure of berrying plants of both sexes must be available. They do well in any ordinary soils.

Many varieties have been raised. Var *crotonifolia*, male, is a fine golden form; *crassifolia*, male, is esteemed for its thick, broad leaves of deep green; *fructu-albo* and *fructu-luteo* are females with whitish and yellowish berries respectively; *longifolia*, a female with narrow leaves, is perhaps the most free in berrying; *nana rotundifolia* is more dwarf and compact, and berries well, and *viridis* is a fine form with fresh unspotted leaves of glossy green.

Propagate very easily from cuttings in summer.

Berberis
Family BERBERIDACEAE

Berberis aggregata

Some of the most rewarding and easily grown shrubs come from this genus of 450 species, with spring flowers, autumn fruits, and attractive foliage. The leaves alternate and are simple, the stems are armed with spines, usually in threes, the flowers yellowish, and the fruits seeded berries. They thrive in sun or partial shade and in almost any soil which is reasonably well drained.

Most deciduous Barberries are Asiatic in origin, fully hardy, and usually have obovate leaves and red berries. The more notable include: *B. aggregata* (western China), 1·2 m (4 ft), clustered yellow flowers in July, small red fruits; *B.* × *carminea* (hybrid), 1·2 m (4 ft), yellow flowers in May, carmine, oval fruits; related forms are 'Fireflame', 'Barbarossa', 'Buccaneer', 'Pirate King'; *B. jamesiana* (Yunnan), 2·1 m (7 ft), racemes of yellow flowers in May, red berries; *B. thunbergii* (Japan), 1·8 m (6 ft), flowers with reddish sepals in April, red berries, and its var *atropurpurea* for foliage colour; *B. wilsonae* (western China), 0·9 m (3 ft), clustered golden-yellow flowers in May and June, coral-red berries; and *B. montana* of the Andes, to 3 m (10 ft), with large flowers.

Propagate by cuttings of firm, ripe shoots in August or by layering for specimens to type; seeds generally give hybrid plants.

Berberis
Family BERBERIDACEAE

Berberis × lologensis

The evergreen Barberries have leathery leaves, often lance-shaped and toothed, with blue, black or purple fruits. The majority are Asiatic, a few South American. Culture and propagation are the same as for deciduous species.

B. darwinii (Chile), 2·4 m (8 ft), racemes of orange yellow flowers in April and May, then dark purple fruits, has several forms, and *B. × irwinii* is a related hybrid with dwarf dense habit. What is listed as *B. gagnepainii* is really its var *lanceifolia* (China), 1·2 m (4 ft), narrow, holly-like leaves, clusters of bright yellow flowers in May and June, then small, blue-black, egg-shaped fruits. *B. julianae* (China), 3 m (10 ft), has narrow, spiny-toothed leaves, clustered bright yellow flowers in May, the blue-black oblong fruits; *B. linearifolia* (Chile), 1·2 m (4 ft), has entire leaves, clustered apricot flowers in May, then blue-black fruits, and a var 'Jewel', even more striking with red flowers. *B × lologensis*, a fine hybrid, has fine sprays of apricot flowers in April and May, then oval fruits. *B. × stenophylla*, also hybrid, up to 2·4 m (8 ft), has clusters of golden-yellow flowers in profusion in April, then black berries with blue bloom; it has many vars of which *coccinea*, *compacta* and *corallina* are excellent small shrubs.

Betula
Family BETULACEAE

Betula nana

The shrubs of the Birch group are chiefly valuable for their pleasing foliage and neat habit. The leaves are alternate and straight-veined; the flowers are unisexual, but on the same (monoecious) plant, with the female catkins appearing at the end of shoots in spring, and the male being formed in the leaf-axils in autumn to open in spring. The seeds are minute nutlets with a pair of transparent wings.

The gem for the shrub garden is *B. nana*, a very hardy native of Britain, Europe and north Asia, slow-growing, of 60–120 cm (2–4 ft) in height, with erect branches, finely downy, and circular, round-toothed, short-stalked leaves, a glossy dark green above, attractively net-veined beneath, and small erect female catkins in April. It is happy in any loamy soil, and thoroughly at home in a damp situation. *B. humilis*, of Europe, up to 2·8 m (9 ft), is neat and small-leaved; and *B. pumila*, of North America, grows erectly to 2·4 m (8 ft), with toothed leaves and downy shoots.

Propagation is best done by seeds which only need to be pressed into the soil, without covering, in February or March.

Butterfly Bush

Buddleia
Family LOGANIACEAE

Buddleia davidii

The beauty of the Buddleias lies in their flowers grouped in rounded panicles or long tapering spikes, attractive to butterflies. The stems are ribbed or angular, the leaves usually opposite, and growth is vigorous in any good loam soil and sunny situation.

Most widely grown is *B. davidii* of China, up to 4·5 m (15 ft) tall, with orange-eyed liliac, scented flowers; and fine vars in 'Black Knight', deep violet; 'Empire Blue', violet blue; 'Royal Red', red purple; and 'White Profusion', pure white; and a form, *nanhoensis*, dainty and elegant at 1·3–2·1 m (5–7 ft) high. *B. fallowiana*, of China, grows 1·2–2·4 m (4–8 ft) tall, and is slender-stemmed and silvery leafed, with fragrant, lavender blue flowers in July; it has a white var, *alba*. The above species and their varieties benefit by being pruned in late winter. *B. alternifolia*, from China, has the habit of a weeping willow, with alternate leaves, and scented lilac flowers in summer. *B. globosa* is a semi-evergreen from South America, 3·0–4·5 m (10–15 ft), with wrinkled and netted leaves, and bright yellow, densely packed flowers in marble-sized balls in June.

Propagate from seeds in early spring, or take late summer cuttings of short side-shoots.

Buxus
Family BUXACEAE

Buxus sempervirens

The sparkling green foliage and neat habit of this group of evergreen small trees and shrubs provide background for showier plants in the shrub garden. The leaves grow opposite, leathery and entire, the flowers, beloved by bees, are yellowish-green, without petals, inconspicuous, and unisexual, growing in axillary clusters in April; the stems are squarish. All species are very hardy, succeeding in any rich soil, particularly chalk, and shaded situations.

B. microphylla, from Japan, is of neat, rounded shape up to 122 cm (4 ft) tall, carrying small, bright green leaves, and terminal clusters of small flowers. *B. sempervirens*, the common Box native to Britain, Europe, North Africa and northern Asia, may be grown as a shrub, a clipped specimen or hedge, or as a bushy tree of 3–6 m (10–20 ft). The leaves are ovate, dark glossy green, the flowers pale green with yellow anthers. Of the varieties, *argentea*, leaves with white border, *aureo-variegata*, leaves mottled yellow, and *aurea pendula*, its weeping golden form, *elegantissima*, silver-margined leaves, dwarf-growing, *handsworthiensis*, upright, *prostrata*, horizontal branching or ground cover, and *suffruticosa*, the edging Box, are worthy of note.

Propagate by cuttings with a heel or by layers in summer.

Heather: Ling

Calluna
Family ERICACEAE

Calluna vulgaris var 'H. E. Beale'

The single representative of this genus is *C. vulgaris*, the Heather or Ling; it grows wild throughout northern Europe, Asia Minor and eastern North America. It is a dwarf evergreen bush, of 10–60 cm (4–24 in), with dark purple-brown gaunt branches and shoots which are clothed with opposite, minute, scale-like linear leaves, arranged in four rows. The flowers are purplish-pink, with a corolla that persists, and they appear in thin terminal spikes from late June to September. They need a lime-free soil. Acid sands, peaty loams or silts are suitable, with good drainage.

Among the finer forms are: var *alba*, the White Heather; *alba plena*, with double flowers; *aurea*, 30 cm (12 in), golden foliage; 'County Wicklow', prostrate habit, double pink flowers; 'C. W. Nix', dwarf, bright crimson flowers; *elegantissima*, 60 cm (24 in), soft lilac flowers; *Foxii*, very dwarf, pink flowers; 'H. E. Beale', 30–45 cm (12–18 in), double pink flowers; 'J. H. Hamilton', 23 cm (9 in), double pink flowers; 'Peter Sparsens', double pink; *serlei*, late, white flowers and its vars *aurea* and *rubra*.

Propagate by dividing plants in April; by cuttings of young shoots in May. Prune by clipping or cutting back previous year's growth in spring, before new growth begins.

Camellia
Family THEACEAE

Camellia japonica var 'Mme Mandal'

A genus of handsome evergreen shrubs with alternate, simple, toothed, ovate leaves of rich green, and flowers of a showy perfection. Although from sub-tropical Asia, and the East, many species and varieties have proved hardy, though it is best to plant in partial shade, sheltered from east winds, and morning sun. They like acid soil; otherwise good drainage and humus richness suits them well.

Hardiest is *C. japonica* from Japan and Korea, 1·3–9 m (5–30 ft), with single flowers of deep scarlet with a boss of yellow stamens, in April to June. There are many forms such as *elegans*, double, carmine rose; 'Gloire de Nantes', semi-double, pink; *magnoliaeflora*, semi-double blush pink; *mathotiana*, double, rose-red; 'Adolphe Audusson', semi-double, crimson; and *nobilissima*, double, white.

C. sasanqua, Japan, 1·2–4·8 m (4–16 ft), bears its single white blooms from January, and needs a protecting wall as does *C. saluenensis*, China, with three-inch flowers of white or rose in March. *C. japonica* × *C. saluenensis* are parents of a new race of free-flowering hybrids, such as 'J. C. Williams' 'Mary Christian', pink; 'Donation', semi-double pink; and others.

Propagate from cuttings of nearly ripe wood in August, in a propagating case or greenhouse, or by layering in September.

Trumpet Flower

Campsis
Family BIGNONIACEAE

Campsis radicans

Two deciduous shrubs climbing by aerial roots and with opposite, pinnate leaves made up of ovate, toothed and pointed leaflets, and large orange-red trumpet-shaped flowers in terminal clusters or panicles, are hardy for the south and south-west of Britain, and should be given good loamy soil and a sunny, warm position.

The hardier of the two is *C. radicans* (syn. *Tecoma radicans*), the Trumpet Flower of the USA, growing to 9 m (30 ft) high, clinging by aerial roots, though some support is helpful, with bright green, pinnate leaves, and producing trumpet-shaped flowers, 7·5 cm (3 in) long, 4 cm (1·5 in) wide, of bright orange-red, in terminal clusters of four to twelve, during August and September. The Chinese *C. grandiflora* (syn *Tecoma chinensis*), grows to 6 m (20 ft), but with few aerial roots, and flowers of deep orange and red in panicles of six to twelve, from July to September. Crossing the two species has given hybrids under *C.* × *tagliabuana* of which 'Madame Galen' with salmon-red flowers is fairly hardy.

Propagate by cuttings in July; by root cuttings in spring. Prune, if needed, in February, cutting back secondary shoots to within a few buds of their base.

Caryopteris
Family VERBENACEAE

Caryopteris × clandonensis

The deciduous shrubs of this genus make a lovely show of colour in late summer with numerous small two-lipped flowers in shades of blue produced freely in branched cymes from the axils and ends of the current season's shoots. The young stems are downy, and the opposite, short-stalked, ovate, often toothed, leaves are a soft dullish green above, grey-white felted below. They like a well-drained sandy loam and a sunny position.

C. incana (syn *C. mastacanthus*), the 'Blue Spiraea' or Moustache plant, of China and Japan, grows 0·9–1·3 m (3–5 ft); its leaves are coarsely toothed, and flowers violet-blue in rounded axillary clusters in September. *C. mongholica*, Mongolia, is also rather tender, growing 0·6–0·9 m (2–3 ft) tall, with linear, entire leaves, downy on both sides, and blue flowers in July and August. Hybrids of the above species, *C. × clandonensis*, and its forms 'Arthur Simmons', 'Ferndown' and 'Heavenly Blue' grow to 0·6–1·2 m (2–4 ft), with soft grey-green leaves, and with branching trusses of bright blue flowers from the leaf-axils and ends of shoots in August and September.

Propagate by cuttings taken in May and June, or by seed. Prune annually in spring, cutting back shoots of the previous year's growth to just above suitable buds.

Cassiope
Family ERICACEAE

Cassiope tetragona

Cassiope (syn *Andromeda*) is a group of hardy, low-growing, evergreen shrubs, with minute, opposite, overlapping, scale-like leaves, lining the stems in four rows, and solitary, nodding, bell-like flowers in April and May. They are found in alpine or arctic regions, and need a lime-free, moist peaty soil, and a situation away from bright direct sun.

The tallest species and the most easy to grow is *C. tetragona*, which sends up tufts of erect stems, 30 cm (12 in) high, closely packed with the deep-green leaves, and bearing small solitary, white, bell-shaped flowers, nodding on slender stems and sometimes tinged pink. *C. fastigata* of the Himalaya is also uprightish, 15–23 cm (6–9 in), the squarish shoots being of closely imbricated green leaves, grooved on the back, and the solitary white flowers being comparatively large. *C. lycopodioides*, from north-east Asia, is just a prostrate mat of squarish leaved, thread-like branches, 2·5 cm (1 in) or so high, with little white bells of flowers in May. *C. mertensiana*, from Alaska, is more erect, to 25 cm (10 in), with white flowers, in April and May; and *C. selaginoides*, from Himalaya, is of tufted erect habit, with white or pinkish flowers.

Propagate by seeds in October, by cuttings in July, by layering in spring.

Ceanothus
Family RHAMNACEAE

Ceanothus × 'Gloire de Versailles'

This genus of some fifty species of shrubs, native to North America, particularly to California, is of special interest for the blueness of its flowers, which, although individually tiny, are numerous in small clusters forming showy spikes or umbels. Some are deciduous, others evergreen. All love the sun, and the evergreens particularly need wall shelter to avoid winter injury. A well drained soil, humus-rich and tending to lightness, is generally suitable.

The best hardy deciduous types are hybrids 1·8–2·4 m (6–8 ft) tall, with large, alternate, three-veined leaves, such as deep blue flowering 'Gloire de Versailles', 'Henri Desfosse', 'Topaz'; pink 'Ceres', 'Perle Rose', and 'Marie Simon'. Among the small-leaved evergreens, *C* × *burkwoodii*, up to 2·4 m (8 ft), with oval, glossy leaves and rich blue flowers, July to October, is hardy; but others, *C. dentatus*, 1·2–2 m (4–6 ft), rich blue, May, and its var *impressus*; *C. thyrsiflorus*, to 9 m (30 ft), pale blue, May and June, are Californian, and need the shelter of a sunny wall.

Propagate by cuttings in late summer; or by layering, spring or autumn. Prune evergreen wall shrubs immediately after flowering, others in March.

Leadwort

Ceratostigma
Family PLUMBAGINACEAE

Ceratostigma willmottianum

The few shrubs of this genus are native to China, with alternate entire leaves that are bristly with forward-facing hairs, and bright blue, five-petalled spreading flowers in terminal heads throughout late summer. The plants are easily grown in light loams, given full sun.

The best type is *C. willmottianum*, making bushy growth 0·6–1·2 m (2–4 ft) high, of angled shoots with stalkless, deciduous, diamond-shaped and pointed leaves, and 5–7·5 cm (2–3 in) wide cluster of bright plumbago-blue flowers from the leaf axils and ends of shoots from the end of July to October. Growth may be killed to ground level in severe winters, but this should be cut away in April, and new growth breaks readily from the base. *C. griffithii* comes from the Himalaya, usually behaves as a deciduous shrub, growing to 1·3 m (5 ft), with bristly shoots, short-pointed obovate leaves of a dull green with reddish-purple margins and small terminal clusters of bright blue flowers in August and September. It should be given a sunny, hot position against a wall with a soil that is not too rich.

Propagate by cuttings with a heel in July and August or by division in March.

Chaenomeles
Family ROSACEAE

Chaenomeles speciosa

The species of this genus of deciduous shrubs are now distinguished from *Cydonia* by having toothed leaves and flower styles united at the base. Beautiful for their early flowers, they are fully hardy, easily cultivated and only need full sun and a reasonably good loam soil.

The popular Japanese Quince is now *C. speciosa* (syn *Cydonia japonica*). It grows from 0·9–3 m (6–10 ft) tall, is of dense, spreading habit, and has spiny branches with ovate, alternate, glossy, green leaves. It bears clusters of bright red flowers, one and a half inches across, in March and April, followed by yellowish-green, rounded fruits. Fine varieties include *nivalis*, pure white; and *moerloesii*, rose and white.

C. japonica (syn *Cydonia maulei*) grows low, to 0·9 m (3 ft), and spreading, with rounded leaves, orange-red flowers, then fragrant yellow fruits; its var *alpina* is more dwarf with brick-red flowers, and *alba* has white. Crossing the two species gave a hybrid race, *C. × superba* of which outstanding vars are 'Crimson and Gold' flowering deep crimson with golden anthers; 'Knap Hill Scarlet', bright orange-scarlet; 'Nicoline', scarlet-red; and 'Rowallane', with large blood-red blooms.

Propagate by layering in spring by suckers planted out in autumn, or by seeds in March.

Winter Sweet

Chimonanthus
Family CALYCANTHACEAE

Chimonanthus praecox

Only one species of this genus is believed to be in cultivation, the Chinese Winter Sweet, *C. praecox* (syns *fragrans, Calycanthus praecox and Meratia praecox*). It is a deciduous shrub making a bush up to 1·8 m (6 ft) tall, though it is probably most satisfactory grown against a wall.

Its greatest charm lies in the translucent, waxlike, many-petalled flowers, usually facing downward on short stalks from old wood, singly or in pairs, with outer petals of pale yellow, and smaller inner petals stained purple, opening to 2·5 cm (1 in) across on the bare shoots between November and March, and having sweet scent. The foliage is of opposite leaves, ovate and long-pointed, up to 18 cm (7 in), and a deep lustrous green. Var *grandiflorus* is more vigorous, producing larger flowers, while the flowers of var *luteus* are primrose-yellow throughout, sweetly scented, and abundantly produced.

Propagate by layering in May. Prune immediately after flowering in early March, shortening flowered shoots back close to base, and removing all weakly growth. In the open, no pruning is needed. A sunny site and reasonably good loam suit.

Chionanthus
Family OLEACEAE

Chionanthus retusus

The two deciduous shrubs in this group make exceptionally beautiful plants, perfectly hardy, thriving in good loam soil and in open positions. The leaves grow opposite or almost so, and are entire and tapering to the base. The loose panicles of pure white flowers with four narrow petals are freely produced.

C. virginicus, the American Fringe Tree, makes a shrub of 3–4·5 m (10–15 ft) high, in Britain and Western Europe, with long, pointed oblong, ovate leaves, and drooping panicles, packed with white flowers having petals 2·5 cm (1 in) long, hanging like a fringe below the branches.

In autumn, the foliage yellows gloriously, and egg-shaped, dark blue berries may appear. The Chinese Fringe Tree, *C. retusus*, grows to 3 m (10 ft), with smaller ovate leaves, and terminal panicles of the snow-white, strap-like petalled flowers in late June and July, with dark blue berries to follow, under favourable conditions.

It is important to get specimens on their own roots, and not grafted or budded stock, if the plants are to remain robust and in flowering vigour for life.

Propagate by seeds. Young plants are slow to flower.

Mexican Orange Blossom

Choisya
Family RUTACEAE

Choisya ternata

A genus of one species, a most charming evergreen shrub from Mexico, *C. ternata*, which has proved to have a certain degree of hardiness for our gardens, remarkable in a plant of so warm a land.

It makes a rounded bush of 1·8–3 m (6–10 ft), clothed in opposite, trifoliolate leaves, made up of three entire, glossy green, obovate leaves, tapering to a sessile or almost stalkless base, and giving a strong but unpleasant aroma when crushed. The flowers are white, five-petalled, and 2·5 cm (1 in) across, and are borne in clusters of four to six from the leaf-axils and the ends of shoots, spreading a hawthorn-like scent through the air. The main flowering period is April and May but intermittent earlier or later blooming is not infrequent.

While the shrub is hardy enough to survive the average frosts, it should be given a warm, sunny position to mature its wood fully, and afforded some shelter from searing easterly winds which damage the foliage. It makes an excellent wall shrub, and its tidy shapeliness makes it a good doorway plant on the south side of a house. Good drainage and a light loam suit it perfectly.

Propagate by cuttings of half-ripe shoots in June.

Cistus
Family CISTACEAE

Cistus × 'Silver Pink'

From warm regions of the Mediterranean, this group of evergreen shrubs with opposite, entire leaves and rose-like flowers in May and June, are of dubious hardiness in severe winters. But they flower freely and grow fast and can be kept in being by simple propagation.

The best of the species are *C. albidus* with hoary foliage, and pale rose-lilac June flowers, of compact growth to 0·9 m (3 ft); *C. ladanifer*, the Gum Cistus, 0·9–1·3 m (3–5 ft), with clammy linear-lanceolate leaves, and 10 cm (4 in) single white flowers, blood red at the base; *C. laurifolius*, 1·8–2·4 m (6–8 ft), with white flowers, yellow at the base, of good hardiness. Among the hybrids are *C.* × 'Silver Pink', to 75 cm (2·5 ft), silver-grey leaves, and 8 cm (3 in) silver-pink flowers; *C.* × *corbariensis*, 60–90 cm (2–3 ft), white flowering; *C.* × *pulverulentus*, (syn *C. crispus*) 60 cm (2 ft), deep rose-pink flowers; *C.* × *cyprius*, 2 m (6·5 ft), clusters of white flowers, crimson blotched; *C.* × *purpureus*, 90 cm (3 ft), large reddish-purple flowers, chocolate blotched at base; and *C.* × *skanbergii*, about 1·2 m (4 ft), with pale rose-pink flowers in clusters.

All need a light, sandy soil and full sun. Propagate by cuttings in August in cold frame or greenhouse.

Clematis
Family RANUNCULACEAE

Clematis × jackmanii

The woody climbing Clematis clamber through and over tall shrubs and trees, as well as up supports placed for them. The leaves are opposite, usually compound, and in the flowers it is the sepals, not the petals, that are showy. All like humus-rich, well drained soil, and do not mind lime. A short list is: *C. armandii*, China, evergreen, to 6 m (20 ft), white flowers, April; *C.* × *jackmanii*, violet-blue flowers, summer; 'Comtesse de Bouchard', soft mauvish-pink; *henryi*, white, summer; *C. macropetala*, China, deciduous, blue-flowering, May, June; *C. montana*, Himalaya, grows to 8 m (26 ft), deciduous, white flowers, May, June; var *grandiflora* is even finer; 'Lasurstern', deep purplish-blue; 'Nelly Moser', mauve-pink, carmine striped, flowering May, June; while 'The President', deep violet, flowers July to October. *C. tangutica*, China, deciduous, 3 m (10 ft), has rich yellow flowers in July; 'Lady Betty Balfour', rich violet-blue; and 'Ville de Lyon', carmine red, late summer.

Propagate by layering, or internodal cuttings taken July or August.

Prune plants that flower on previous season's growth after flowering; those that bloom on shoots of current growth in February.

Clerodendrum
Family VERBENACEAE

Clerodendrum bungei

Most of the 300 species of *Clerodendrum* (often *Clerodendron*) inhabit hot regions of Africa and the East Indies, and only a few have sufficient hardiness for outdoors in Britain. These are deciduous shrubs with large, opposite leaves, and the showy clusters of deliciously fragrant flowers that earn the common name of Glory Tree or Glory Bower. They are eligible for favoured gardens which are sunny and warm and well sheltered from east wind and spring frosts, with decent loam soil, freely enriched with peat.

The hardiest is possibly *C. fargesii* (syn *C. trichotomum* var *fargesii*), upright and strong-growing to 3·7 m (12 ft), with long, ovate leaves, and clusters of starry, white scented flowers in August, followed by porcelain blue berries cradled in persistent crimsoning calyces. *C. bungei* is usually winter-cut to the ground, but sends up a thicket of erect shoots 0·9–1·2 m (3–4 ft), with large, toothed, heart-shaped leaves of unpleasant smell when crushed, but the terminal rounded clusters of tightly packed purplish-red flowers appearing in August and September are sweetly fragrant. All come from China.

Propagate by root cuttings in April or by rooted suckers. *C. bungei* can be divided.

Clethra
Family Clethraceae

Clethra delavayi

A genus of woody plants, some deciduous, some evergreen, valued for their late summer flowering. The leaves are alternate, toothed and prominently veined, and the flowers are borne in racemes or panicles and are highly scented. They do best in lime-free soils, well-drained, but humus-rich.

C. alnifolia, the Sweet Pepper-bush of east North America, is a hardy deciduous shrub of upright branching habit to 3 m (10 ft), with short-pointed, obovate leaves, and erect, spreading sprays of strongly scented white flowers, July to September. *C. tomentosa* of south-east USA, is also a deciduous shrub, 2·4 m (8 ft) tall, and similar in character, but with very downy young shoots and more spreading flowers. Of the Chinese species, *C. delavayi* is the gem for mild gardens, making an erect, large, deciduous bush or small tree, covered with crowded racemes of cup-shaped white flowers in July and August. *C. barbinervis*, Japan, makes a big bush of beauty, with downy racemes, 23 cm (9 in) long, of very fragrant small white flowers in July and August.

Propagate by layering, in spring or by heeled cuttings in July and August, or by seed in spring.

Colutea
Family LEGUMINOSAE

Colutea arborescens

This race of deciduous shrubs from southern Europe and the Mediterranean region is colourful and interesting. They have the pinnate, alternate leaves so typical of the Pea family, bear pea-like, yellow or yellowish-red flowers in long-stalked racemes in summer, and large, inflated, bladder-like pods with whitish papery walls in autumn. They are quite hardy, and especially suitable for poor soil.

C. arborescens is characteristic of the genus, a vigorous shrub of rounded habit, growing up to 3·7 m (12 ft). The leaves are made up of nine to thirteen oval leaflets, notched at the apex, and the flowers are bright yellow, in clusters from the leaf-axils, from June to October; the bladder-pods are 7·5 cm (3 in) long. *C. orientalis* is of rounded compact habit, growing 1·2–1·27 m (4–5 ft), with grey-green leaves with rounded leaflets, and racemes of coppery-red flowers, followed by 3.5 cm (1·5 in) pods with open ends. *C.* × *media*, a hybrid of *C. arborescens* × *C. orientalis*, has flowers of a bronze or orange-red and, later, 7 cm (3 in) pods.

Propagate from half-ripe shoots in July, or by seeds. Prune in February, cutting forward wood back almost to the base.

Convolvulus
Family CONVOLVULACEAE

Convolvulus cneorum

This genus, although containing some notoriously pernicious weeds, also provides many handsome flowering plants, among them a rather beautiful and striking shrub, *C. cneorum*. This native of southern Europe grows from about 45–95 cm (1·5–3 ft) high, and as much across, with branching stems, dressed with evergreen, lanceolate leaves, 5 cm (2 in) long, tapering at the base, all covered with silvery-silky hairs, giving a silvery, shining, blue-green appearance to the whole plant. The flowers are trumpet-shaped, white or pale pink, hairy on the outside, and are borne in terminal clusters opening successively over a long period from May onwards. It makes a very decorative plant, especially for sunny borders and banks. Its only drawback is that it is only hardy enough for warm gardens in the south, where it should be given a hot sunny spot, and a well drained loam soil which may contain lime or not.

Propagate by cuttings in June in a propagating case.

Cornus
Family CORNACEAE

Cornus kousa

The shrubs of this genus are deciduous, with opposite, entire, pointed leaves, with well-marked parallel veins, and four-parted flowers. They may be grouped into those with well-bracted flowers, and those without bracts. All grow well in ordinary garden soils.

Of the first group, are *C. kousa*, from Japan, a tall elegant shrub to 6 m (19 ft), with small, creamy-white bracted flowers in June, and its var *chinensis* with larger bracts; *C. mas*, the Cornelian Cherry of Europe, a hardy shrub up to 4·5 m (15 ft), with clusters of yellow flowers in small bracts appearing in February before the leaves, and its golden, and silver variegated vars; and *C. nuttallii*, western North America, a May-flowering tall shrub of 4·5–8 m (15–25 ft), with small flowers, and four to eight creamy-white bracts, flushing pink later. All have autumn foliage colour.

Of the second group, *C. alba*, of Siberia, a spreading shrub to 3 m (10 ft) high, is esteemed for the redness of its stems in winter; var *atrosanguinea* being more dwarfed and crimson and var *sphaethii* has finely golden variegated leaves.

Propagate by layering in spring, or by cuttings of firm shoots in autumn, or by suckers.

Corylopsis
Family HAMAMELIDACEAE

Corylopsis spicata

The great charm of the deciduous shrubs of this genus lies in the soft, pure beauty and fragrance of the clear yellow flowers, with bracts at their base, produced in drooping sprays on the leafless shoots in spring. The foliage is of alternate leaves with strong parallel veins, finely toothed, and more or less heart-shaped at the base. All are hardy and easily grown in soils rich in organic matter and well drained.

C. pauciflora from Japan makes a small, rounded shrub with many twiggy branches, 0·9–2 m (3–6·5 ft) high, from which dangle open primrose-yellow flowers with creamy-green bracts in clusters of two or three, sweetly scented, in March and April. *C. spicata*, also from Japan, is a spreading shrub, up to 2 m (6·5 ft), with 3·5 cm (1·5 in) long, drooping sprays of six to twelve yellow, fragrant flowers in March and April, and 10 cm (4 in) long roundish, cordate leaves later. China gives us *C. sinensis*, a large shrub to 4·5 m (15 ft) high, with lemon-yellow scented flowers, twelve or more to the spike; *C. platypetala*, a shrub of 1·8 m (6 ft), with flower spikes 5–7·5 cm (2–3 in) long; and *C. willmottiae*, up to 3 m (10 ft), having up to twenty soft yellow flowers per spike.

Propagate by layering in March; by cuttings with a heel in July and August.

Cotoneaster
Family ROSACEAE

Cotoneaster salicifolius

This genus has given us many worthwhile shrubs for our gardens, varying in size, ornamental qualities and attractiveness. They are characterized by somewhat spreading growth, hairy branchlets, and entire, stiffish leaves, alternate or in clusters, short-stalked and woolly beneath. The small white or pinkish flowers are borne solitary or in clusters, usually in May and June, followed by seed fruits which are often a valuable ornament to the autumn-winter scene. For hardiness and easy culture, they are hard to excel, and while flourishing at their best in good loams, they also succeed in poor soils, lime or peat.

Of deciduous sorts, *C. bullatus*, western China, 1·8–3 m (6–10 ft), is outstanding for its rugged leaves and brilliant red fruits. *C. horizontalis*, with its fish-bone branches lined with red berries well into the winter, is essential for walls, banks and north aspects. *C. divaricatus*, western China, to 1·8 m (6 ft), spreads widely, foliage colours finely in autumn, and fruits are scarlet. *C. salicifolius*, China, to 3·7 m (12 ft), is variable, often evergreen with willow-like leaves and red fruits. *C. adpressus*, China, is a prostrate spreading shrub, 30 cm (12 in) high, of value in clothing banks and rocks.

Cotoneaster
Family ROSACEAE

Cotoneaster franchettii

Evergreen Cotoneaster add foliage beauty to colourful berrying habits, and grow in most garden soils; and in most aspects.

The best tall growers are the hybrids of *C. frigidus*: *C.* × 'Cornubia', 6·5 m (20 ft) or more, with long, lance-shaped leaves, large white flower clusters, yielding to drooping big, bright red fruits; *C.* × *watereri*, a large shrub, up to 6·5 m (20 ft) or so, with large leaves and masses of large red berries. *C. franchettii*, China, spreads gracefully, 2·4 m (8 ft), with small, grey-green leaves, pinkish flower clusters in May and pear-like, orange-scarlet fruits later. From China also comes *C. lacteus*, to 3·7 m (12 ft), long oval leaves milky-grey beneath, and clusters of fine red fruits. *C. simonsii*, Himalaya, not always fully evergreen, grows erect to 3 m (10 ft) and carries orange-red berries in autumn. *C. wardii*, Tibet, upright and arching, may grow to 2·4 m (8 ft) tall, with shining small leaves, colouring in autumn, and orange-red fruits, and is a fine species. *C. microphyllus*, 0·9 m (3 ft), but spreading, is good for covering banks; *C. conspicuus*, Tibet, 1·2–1·27 m (4–5 ft), flowers prettily, and is red-berrying. *C. dammeri*, China, is a prostrate carpeter.

Propagate all Cotoneasters by seeds, or by cuttings taken in later summer.

Cytisus
Family LEGUMINOSAE

Cytisus scoparius var *fulgens*

A group of quick-growing, colourful and generally deciduous shrubs. The stems are slender, green and ribbed, with alternate, simple or trifoliolate leaves, pea-shaped flowers, and podded seeds which have a warty appendage characteristic of the genus. They do well in any good well-drained loam soil, love full sun, and do best planted out of pots to avoid root injury.

Dwarf kinds include *C. demissus*, Mediterranean, a brief 5–7·5 cm (2–3 in), with yellow, tinged reddish-brown flowers in May and June; *C. decumbens*, from southern Europe, prostrate stems and shining yellow flowers in May and June; *C. ardoinii*, French Alps, 15 cm (6 in), upright branching, with butter-yellow flowers in April and May, and hybrids, *C.* × *beanii*, 30 cm (12 in), deep yellow flowers, and *C.* × *kewensis*, 45 cm (18 in), with creamy-yellow flowers, in May. *C. albus* is the white Broom of Spain and Portugal, upright to 3 m (10 ft). *C. scoparius*, the common Broom, 1·8 m (6 ft), is at its best in its vars, *andreanus*, yellow and crimson; 'Daisy Hill', sulphur-yellow; 'Firefly', red-brown and gold; 'Golden Sunlight', bright yellow; and *sulphureus*, sulphur-yellow.

Propagate by seeds or summer cuttings.

Daboecia
Family ERICACEAE

Daboecia cantabrica var *alba*

This small genus contains two species; both are neat, evergreen shrubs, with alternate lanceolate leaves, 12·7 mm (0·5 in) long, and egg-shaped flowers in erect, terminal racemes, over a long period. Given a lime-free loam soil, they are easily grown and need little attention.

St. Dabeoc's Heath, the Irish and Connemara Heath, botanically *D. cantabrica*, is found in western France, Spain, Portugal and the Azores as well as in Ireland. It makes a dense, compact shrub of 0·3–0·9 m (1–3 ft) in height, with recurving, dark glossy green leaves, white felted beneath, and upright racemes, 7·5–15 cm (3–6 in) long, of large, rose-purple, hanging, egg-shaped flowers from May to September. Var *alba* is a most charming white-flowering form found in Connemara. Var *atropurpurea* has flowers of deeper, richer purple than the type. There is a dwarf variety, *nana*, with smaller leaves and smaller flowers. *D. azorica*, from the Azores, is rather less hardy and needs mild conditions, but it makes a low, compact evergreen shrub of 10–20 cm (4–8 in), with ruby-crimson flowers in June and July.

Propagate by layers in spring or autumn; by cuttings in June to August; or by seeds.

Daphne
Family THYMELAEACEAE

Daphne mezereum

Although providing some of the most beautiful and most sweetly scented of shrubs, the Daphnes are apt to prove capricious to grow. They make small to medium-sized shrubs, with alternate, entire leaves, small flowers with a petal-like, four-lobed calyx, and small, one-seeded berries. They thrive best in humus-rich soils which are well-drained and cool. Plant young, leave undisturbed.

The cottage Mezereon, *D. mezereum*, well-known native of Europe, making a globular bush, 0·6–1·27 m (2–5 ft) tall, with finely scented, lilac-pink to purplish-red flowers crowding the stems between November and March, before the grey-green leaves appear, is still the best, with red berries later which can be propagated. Var *alba* is a white-flowering form, and *grandiflora* has larger flowers. *D. cneorum*, the Garland Flower, also European, is evergreen, 30 cm (12 in) high, with scented, rose-pink flowers in May, and has white var *alba* and other forms. *D.* × *burkwoodii* 'Somerset', to 0·9 m (3 ft), flowers bluish-pink, in June. *D. bholua*, Himalaya, up to 2 m (6·5 ft), is rare but good.

Propagate by layering shoots in autumn; or by sowing seeds as soon as they are ripe.

Desfontainea
Family POTALIACEAE

Desfontainea spinosa

The genus is one of a single species, *Desfontainea spinosa* (syn *D. hookeri*), which comes from the Andes of Chile and Peru, sometimes called 'Chilean Holly'.

It makes a magnificent evergreen shrub, capable of growing up to 3 m (10 ft) high, but usually attaining 0·9–2 m (3–6·5 ft) in our gardens. The leaves grow opposite, and are very like those of holly, but ovate or oval, and a shining, somewhat lighter green, with a spiny edge. The flowers never fail to win admiration, hanging down singly from the shoots, with a funnel-shaped corolla of crimson-scarlet, ending in five yellow-tipped, shallow, flared lobes, from a five-parted green calyx, during July and October. A well-drained, loamy soil is suitable, and a position which affords shade, shelter from drying winds, and ample moisture is appreciated. The plant is hardy enough to be grown without much trouble in most gardens in the west, and in places where the moist conditions of its shady native rain forests can be reproduced.

Propagate by seeds in spring; or by shoot cuttings in June-July, rooted in a shaded propagating case or frame.

Deutzia
Family PHILADELPHACEAE

Deutzia × rosea

The genus is one of deciduous shrubs, with brown, peeling bark, thin, opposite, toothed and fine-pointed leaves with minute, star-like hairs on the surfaces, and clusters or panicles of five-parted flowers freely produced in May, June and July. They will grow in quite poor soils, but prefer a good, moist loam with sound drainage, out of the reach of late spring frosts.

Out of some fifty species and many hybrids, some of the best are *D. × magnifica*, a hybrid, 2–2·4 m (6–8 ft) tall, with rough leaves, and large, erect clusters of double white flowers in June; *D. × rosea*, a hybrid of compact growth, up to 0·9 m (3 ft) tall, with frilled, bell-shaped rose-pink flowers in May; var *grandiflora* being more showy with larger clusters. *D. scabra*, Japan, grows to 3 m (10 ft) with white flowers in big, erect panicles in June and July, and its vars *candidissima*, and *plena*, white flushed rose are good. *D. setchuenensis*, up to 1·2 m (4 ft) and its var *corymbiflora* are fine, late-July, white flowering shrubs; from China.

Propagate by cuttings of half-ripened shoots in July, by division in winter. Prune immediately after flowering or in March.

Oleaster

Elaeagnus
Family ELAEAGNACEAE

Elaeagnus angustifolia

Attractive foliage, fragrant flowers and handsome fruits mark this group of evergreen and deciduous shrubs, the stems and alternate entire leaves being covered with brown or silvery scales. All are hardy and succeed in ordinary soils, under trees or in shade, and are good for planting in seaside gardens.

Of the deciduous kinds, *E. angustifolia*, the Oleaster of Europe and west Asia, grows to 4·5 m (15 ft) or more, with spiny branches, long, narrow, silvery leaves, small yellow scented flowers from the leaf-axils in May, and oval, silver-scaled yellowish edible berries. *E. umbellata*, Himalaya, China and Japan, grows 4·5 m (15 ft), with silvery-white flowers in May or June, and small red berries. Among the evergreens, *E. macrophylla*, Korea and Japan, makes a rounded, wider shrub, 2·4–3 m (8–10 ft), with very fragrant, silvery flowers in October. *E. pungens*, Japan, 3–4·5 m (10–15 ft), with wavy-edged leaves and silvery, scented flowers, October, has variegated vars *maculata*, yellow, *variegata*, cream. *E.* × *ebbingei* is fast growing to 2·4 m (8 ft), and a good windbreak.

Propagate deciduous kinds by seeds, evergreens by cuttings in June and July. Little pruning is needed.

Enkianthus
Family ERICACEAE

Enkianthus campanulatus

This group of deciduous shrubs has two seasons of attraction: spring, when hanging clusters of white or pink bell-shaped flowers grace the ends of shoots; and autumn, when the foliage becomes resplendent in hues of orange and crimson. The plants produce their branches in whorls, with alternate, ovate and finely-toothed leaves, often clustered at the ends, flowering in May or June. They must have a lime-free soil, preferably loamy, and appreciate partial shade.

E. campanulatus of Japan is most commonly available, growing slowly from 1·3–2·8 m (5–9 ft) tall, erect and branching, with drooping racemes of creamy-yellow, lily-of-the-valley-like flowers, veined and flushed red, and bright red foliage in autumn. *E. cernuus*, also of Japan, is rare but fine, with compact growth up to 1·3 m (5 ft), with small, dark green leaves and tight racemes of white flowers, with frilled petals. *E. perulatus*, Japan, makes slow growth to 1·8 m (6 ft), with dense foliage of oval leaves clustering at the ends of shoots, and clusters of urn-shaped, white flowers in May, followed by glorious autumn colouring of orange and red.

Propagate by layering in June, or by cuttings from June to August in cold frame. No pruning normally needed, except of dead wood.

Erica
Family ERICACEAE

Erica arborea

The hardy evergreen shrubs of the Heath genus merit representation everywhere. They have small, linear, blunt-ended leaves, usually whorled, and small, egg-shaped, four-parted flowers in shades of white, pink, or purple, profusely produced and lasting long. All appreciate good drainage and a soil enriched with leafmould or peat.

E. arborea, the Tree Heath, from the Mediterranean, grows to 3 m (10 ft), with greyish leaves in whorls of three, and sweet-scented, white flowers in terminal clusters in March and April. Only hardy for mild localities, its var *alpina*, from Spain, is hardier, and grows only to 1·3–2·4 m (5–8 ft). *E. australis*, the Spanish Heath, grows 1·2–2 m (4–6 ft), with dark green leaves, whorled in fours, and purplish-red flowers in April. The Portuguese Heath, *E. lusitanica*, grows erect and up to 3 m (10 ft), with pale green leaves, and flowers opening white in March to May. *E.* × *veitchii* 'Exeter', to 1·3 m (5 ft) has white, scented flowers opening in February. *E. erigena* (syn *mediterranea*), south-west France and Spain, makes a dense shrub with pink flowers in early spring, up to 1·8 m (6 ft) tall, and has notable vars, such as 'Brightness', bright red flowers; 'W. T. Rackliff', white; *superba*, pink; and *rubra*, red.

Propagate by young shoot cuttings in cold frame in July-August. Prune, when necessary, after flowering.

Erica
Family ERICACEAE

Erica herbacea (syn *carnea*)

The heaths that flower in winter are alpine, hardy, have a tolerance for lime, and can therefore be grown in any soils which drain well, enriched with peat or leafmould. They do well in open situations and as carpeting plants in borders or woodland.

E. herbacea (syn *carnea*) is the chief species from the alps of central Europe. It makes a shrub of 15–30 cm (6–12 in) high, and up to 45 cm (18 in) spread, with smooth, young stems, carrying linear leaves in whorls of four, and urn-shaped, rose-pink flowers, in one-sided racemes, from December into April. Among the best forms are: 'Queen Mary', rich pink, January and February; 'Winter Beauty' ('King George'), deep pink, 'Loughrigg', rose-purple, dark foliage; and *aurea*, pink, golden foliage; from November–December; 'Cecilia M. Beale', a good white with erect habit and early flowering; 'Springwood White', with white flowers and brown anthers, and 'Springwood Pink', with pink flowers; *atro-rubra*, dark crimson; 'Ruby Glow', carmine; 'Eileen Porter', pink, and *vivellii*, dark crimson-red with bronzed foliage, are later flowering. *E.* × *darleyensis* (*E. herbacea* × *E. erigena*) (syn 'Darley Dale') is a rounded shrub of 60 cm (2 ft), pale pink from November to April.

Prune by trimming faded flower shoots in late spring.

Erica
Family ERICACEAE

Erica cinerea var 'Eden Valley'

Summer and autumn ground colour is provided by heaths which may be found growing wild in Britain.

One is *E. cinerea*, variously known as the Bell, or the Grey, or Scotch Heath, a honey plant for bees on our moorlands and throughout western Europe. It makes a shrub from 30–60 cm (12–24 in) tall, with small, recurved, deep green, linear leaves in threes, and large, rosy-purple, urn-shaped flowers borne in sprays at the ends of shoots, from June to September. A lime-free, humus-rich soil is needed. Of varieties, var *alba*, 23–30 cm (9–12 in) tall, with long racemes of pure white flowers; 'Apple Blossom', 30 cm (12 in) tall, with light green leaves and shell-pink flowers; *atrorubens*, ruby-red flowers; 'C. D. Eason', bright red; 'Eden Valley', lilac-pink; 'P. S. Patrick', rich purple; *rosea*, clear, bright pink; are outstanding. *E. ciliaris*, the Dorset Heath, also provides summer and autumn colour, but needs a moist, lime-free soil. It spreads about 30 cm (12 in) high, with small, ovate, hairy or fringed leaves, and bright-pink bell-shaped flowers in threes in sprays 7·5–12·7 cm (3–5 in) long from July into October. The best white variety is 'Stoborough'; *maweana* with large rose-crimson flowers is commendable.

Prune by trimming faded flower shoots in late autumn to early spring.

Erica
Family ERICACEAE

Erica vagans

The Cornish Heath, *E. vagans*, is native to south-west Europe and not reliably hardy. Nevertheless, it adds to the heath colour in summer and autumn, where the soil is lime-free and loamy. It makes a spreading shrub of 0·3–0·9 m (1–3 ft) high, with linear leaves in whorls of four or five, and small, purplish-pink flowers from July to November. Var 'Lyonesse' has clear white flowers with brown anthers; 'Mrs. D. F. Maxwell' has long racemes of warm pink bloom; and 'St Keverne', rose-pink.

The Cross-leaved Heath, *E. tetralix*, grows in north and west Europe, as well as in Britain, and flowers during June to October. It forms a shrub, 15–45 cm (6–18 in) high, with small, hairy leaves, white below, arranged in fours on the stems, and pink, egg-shaped flowers in terminal clusters. Good vars are *alba*, white flowering; *mollis*, white hoary foliage, white flowers; 'Pink Glow', pink flowers; and 'Silver Bells', a dwarf with flowers of a lovely silver-pink. *E.* × *mackayi* (*E. tetralix* × *E. ciliaris*) is dwarf with bright pink flowers, and has vars 'Dawn', deep rose, and 'H. Maxwell', rose-red, of merit.

All the Ericas are easily propagated by cuttings in June to August, rooting freely in peaty soils. Trim after flowering.

Chilean Gum Box

Escallonia
Family ESCALLONIACEAE

Escallonia × edinensis

A genus of evergreen shrubs from South America, chiefly Chile, providing valuable subjects for planting in seaside and windy gardens in mild western localities, and for floral beauty on walls; but discrimination is needed, especially for inland and northern gardens, as hardiness is often suspect. Growth is erect and branching, with finely-toothed alternate leaves, with short or no stalks, and small flowers, five-parted, in terminal panicles or racemes. They will grow in all ordinary garden soils, and like sun.

Of the species, *E. macrantha*, from Chile, growing 1·8–3 m (6–10 ft), densely foliaged with large, shining deep green, toothed leaves, and rose-crimson flowers from June to September, is good for hedges and walls. *E. virgata*, deciduous, lime-intolerant, and hardy, has white flowers, June to August. There are many beautiful hybrids of varied parentage also, of which some notable forms are: 'Apple Blossom', pink and white; 'C. F. Ball', crimson; 'Donard Beauty', rosy-red; 'Donard Brilliance', crimson; *E. × edinensis*, neat, 1·2 m (4 ft), rose-pink; *E. × langleyensis*, rose-crimson; *E. × exoniensis*, white; and *E. × iveyi*, tall white.

Propagate by cuttings in late summer in a propagating case. Prune flowered shoots in autumn.

Eucryphia
Family EUCRYPHIACEAE

Eucryphia glutinosa

Distinctive in habit and foliage, the shrubs of this genus are evergreen or nearly so, with opposite leaves, and bear white, four-petalled flowers, opening like single roses, with a thick brush of anthers. They are somewhat slow coming into flower and tender when young. They are best suited to mild localities of the south-west in the open, and for sheltered walls elsewhere.

The hardiest is *E. gluntinosa* of Chile, making an upright, branching shrub to 4·5 m (15 ft), with shining green, pinnate leaves of three or five oval, toothed leaflets, colouring yellowish in autumn, and 6–7 cm (2·5 in) across at the ends of shoots in August. It needs a lime-free, well-drained, cool soil. Another Chilean, *E. cordifolia*, may grow to 12 m (40 ft), with stiff, dark green, narrow heart-shaped leaves, and clear white flowers in August. Hybrids are *E.* × 'Nymansay', erect, evergreen, and tree-like, to 9 m (30 ft), with yellow-anthered, white flowers, and *E.* × 'Rostrevor', also evergreen and tree-like, to 10·5 m (35 ft), with white flowers in August. All but *E. glutinosa* will grow in free-draining loam soil, containing no more than a modicum of chalk or lime.

Propagate by layers in spring or by cuttings in June. No regular pruning is needed.

Euonymus
Family CELASTRACEAE

Euonymus japonicus var *aureus*

The genus contains widely different shrubs, with opposite, finely-toothed leaves, small flowers in axillary clusters and pendulous fruits, lobed or winged, and brightly coloured. Those named here are hardy, to be grown in almost any soil limy or not.

Of the deciduous sorts, *E. alatus*, the Winged Spindle of China and Japan, is a shrub, slow-growing to 1·8 m (6 ft), with branches having two thin corky wings, oval, dark-green leaves, yellowish June flowers, and lobed purplish fruits, with fine rosy-crimson autumn foliage. *E. europaeus*, the Common Spindle Tree, makes a shrub or tree up to 6 m (20 ft), attractive for its red lobed fruits with orange-coated seeds. *E. latifolius*, Europe, 3–6 m (10–20 ft), is spreading, with rosy-red fruits and rich red autumn leaves. *E. sachalinensis*, 3 m (10 ft), and *E. yedoensis*, 3·6 m (12 ft), are fine autumn colouring species with reddish fruits from Japan. *E. japonicus*, Japan, with oval, evergreen leaves, is used for hedges or as a shrub, up to 3 m (10 ft) or more, and has many forms, golden-silver-variegated and pyramidal. *E. fortunei* and its var *radicans*, Japan, are trailing evergreens for ground cover or walls, and have several related lovely variegated varieties.

Propagate deciduous species by seeds in February, evergreens by cuttings in May and June.

Fabiana
Family SOLANACEAE

Fabiana imbricata

Two charming evergreen species of this South American genus have entered our gardens from Chile. Although heath-like in appearance, with erect and spreading, tapering, downy branches, having numerous short, slender twigs, crowded with alternate, tiny, stiff, scale-like, triangular leaves, and terminating in erect tubular flowers in June, the shrubs are more closely related to the Nightshade and Potato. They are not fully hardy, and therefore only eligible for the open in mild and sheltered gardens, where they thrive in a well-drained, light soil, acid or limy, and abundant sunshine.

F. imbricata grows erect and may attain a height of 2 m (3–6·5 ft). Its branches become heath-like plumes when bearing the white, erect tubular flowers in June. There is a dwarf form, var *prostrata*, with pale mauve flowers with a reputation of greater hardiness. *F. violacea* is a shrub of similar habit to *F. imbricata*, but grows more quickly and not so tall, with flowers that vary in colour from milk-blue to a washy mauve. It is less striking, but reputedly more hardy.

Propagate by cuttings with a heel in late summer under glass. Prune after flowering, if necessary.

Fatsia
Family ARALIACEAE

Fatsia japonica

The genus is one of two species, notable for their large handsome, palmate, evergreen leaves, growing alternate on thick stems, and bearing large panicles of white flowers late in the year.

The better known is *F. japonica* (syn *Aralia sieboldii*), often grown as an indoor or greenhouse plant. But it is hardy enough to be grown out of doors, given a sheltered and fairly well shaded position, and free-draining, loamy soil, and is excellent for seaside planting in the south-west, where it will stand up to the sea winds. This Japanese evergreen gives a bold and tropical look to gardens, and is well suited to terraces, courtyards and formal surroundings. It grows 2·4–3·7 m (8–12 ft) tall, with thickish stems, long, leathery, shining green leaves, palmately lobed, particularly striking when young and unfolding, and branching panicles of milky-white flowers in October. The Chinese *F. papyrifera*, with pithy shoots, and flowers in panicles up to 75 cm (30 in) long at the ends in October, needs the warmth of a sheltered Cornish garden, or a cool greenhouse.

Propagate by root cuttings in March–April, in propagating case, by stem cuttings in summer.

Forsythia
Family OLEACEAE

Forsythia × *intermedia* var *spectabilis*

There are six species in this genus of beautiful, easily grown, spring-flowering, deciduous shrubs. The shoots are four-angled with opposite, simple or trifoliolate leaves, ovate and roughly toothed in outer half, and the yellow flowers burst from lateral buds on wood of the previous year's growth before the leaves unfold. All are hardy, grow in various aspects and in any reasonably well-drained soil.

F. ovata, Korea, a compact shrub of 0·9–1·2 m (3–4 ft), and slow-growing, bears golden-yellow flowers in March. *F. suspensa*, China, spreads wide and tall, to 3 m (10 ft), with golden-yellow flowers in March and April, var *fortunei* is good. *F. viridissima*, east China, grows stiffly erect to 2–2·4 m (6–8 ft), with large, bright yellow flowers in April. Crossed with *F. suspensa*, the last has given us *F.* × *intermedia*, graceful and robust to 3 m (10 ft) tall, with yellow flowers in March, of which forms 'Beatrix Farrand', 'Lynwood', *primulina* and *spectabilis*, are very fine.

Propagate by softwood cuttings taken in July, or cuttings taken with a heel in October. Little or no pruning should be necessary, but if done, cut immediately flowering is over.

Fothergilla
Family HAMAMELIDACEAE

Fothergilla monticola

The genus belongs to the south-eastern states of North America; deciduous shrubs of good habit, with alternate, stalked, obovate leaves, coarsely toothed and flowers without petals but with many, long, conspicuous stamens with white thickened tops, crowded in erect, bottle-brush-like heads appearing before the leaves, and being attractively ornamental. In autumn the leaves turn crimson or orange and pay another dividend of beauty. The shrubs are hardy, but do best in a sandy-peat, acid loam of good drainage and some shade.

F. major is a shrub of 2 m (6·5 ft) or so, with feathery white spikes of fragrant flowers in April, and the foliage colours a rich orange-yellow in autumn. *F. gardenii* (syn *alnifolia*) makes a small shrub 60–90 cm (24–36 in) tall, with sweet-scented spikes of white-stamened flowers in April and May, and small, leaves, colouring crimson in autumn; *F. monticola* grows 0·9–1·2 m (3–5 ft) high, with milk-white flower-brushes in April, and leaves that crimson in the autumn.

Propagate by cuttings taken with a heel in summer, or by seeds in February, though slow-germinating. No regular pruning is needed.

Fuchsia
Family ONAGRACEAE

Fuchsia magellanica

None of the hundred species of this genus are fully hardy for all gardens. They come from Central and South America and New Zealand, and are killed to ground-level in our winter, but some species send up new shoots readily from the base each year, and their fresh green, opposite or whorled leaves, and exotic drooping flowers with long protruding stamens are most welcome for summer and autumn colour. They succeed in any decent loam, welcome partial shade, and do not mind woodland conditions. A covering of leafmould or peat and soil over the crown of the plants ensures survival.

The hardiest plants are *F. megallanica* of southern South America. The type may grow to 2 m (6·5 ft), with bright green, ovate, toothed leaves, and nodding flowers made up of a red tube and four spreading red sepals, purple to blue petals, and eight stamens, June to October, and vars *riccartonnii*, 1·2–2·4 m (4–8 ft), very hardy, free-flowering, red and purple; 'Madame Cornelissen', red sepals, white cupped flower; 'Mrs. Popple', larger flowers. There are also many choice named garden hybrids.

Propagate by cuttings in summer. Prune in spring, cutting previous year's growth hard back.

Silver Tassel Bush

Garrya
Family GARRYACEAE

Garrya elliptica

A group of evergreen shrubs which have ornamental garden value, partly in their foliage made up of opposite, entire, ovate leaves, wavy-margined and dark green with greyish down beneath, but chiefly for their silvery-grey catkins which are made up of small, insignificant flowers within cup-shaped bracts and are unisexual. The shrubs grow freely in any ordinary garden soil, but deserve some shelter from chilling winds and foliage-spoiling frosts. They resent root disturbance and are best planted out of pots, when young, in permanent quarters, preferably on a slope to the south or west, or a sunny wall facing these quarters, with protection against north and east winds.

The hardiest species is *G. elliptica*, from California and Oregon, growing to 1·8–3·7 m (6–12 ft), with oval to roundish leaves, and silver-grey flowering tassels hanging clustered at the ends of shoots, 7·5–15 cm (3–6 in) long, and often longer on male plants, such as var 'James Roof', in mild quarters, while on female trees the catkins are shorter but may hang from November into February.

Propagate by half-ripened cuttings in August. Prune immediately after flowering, if necessary.

Gaultheria
Family ERICAEAE

Gaultheria cuneata

The hardy evergreen shrubs of this genus have much ornamental beauty in their foliage of leathery, alternate leaves, their bell- or urn-shaped flowers, and their berry-like capsular fruits. They need a lime-free soil, preferably humus-rich and well-drained, and appreciate partial shade, or grow in full shade.

G. procumbens is the Canada Tea, Creeping Wintergreen, Checkerberry or Partridge Berry of North America, a creeping shrub with shoots to 15 cm (6 in) high, clustered with small, finely-toothed, ovate leaves to the top, and with solitary, white flushed pink flowers from the leaf-axils in July and August, followed by bright red, rounded fruits. Others of note are *G. cuneata*, western China, a compact shrub of 30 cm (12 in) or so, white-flowering in June, and white-berried later; *G. shallon*, the North American Salal, makes a dense bush, 60–120 cm (2–4 ft) tall, with large, dark green leaves, pale pink bell-flowers in May and June, and purple-black fruits. *G. hookeri*, Himalaya, may grow to 2 m (6·5 ft), bears pink flowers in April, and needs a sheltered site.

Propagate by cuttings taken in August, layering, offsets, or by seeds.

Genista
Family LEGUMINOSAE

Genista hispanica

Like *Cytisus*, a closely related genus, this group of deciduous shrubs is commonly called Broom. The fresh green stems furnished with alternate leaves, and the pea-like flowers, are borne in terminal racemes, giving way to small, linear pods. The species given do well in light, well-drained soils and sunny positions, and are best planted out of pots and left undisturbed.

Tallest are *G. aethnensis*, the Mount Etna Broom, 3–4·5 m (10–15 ft), of Sicily, with masses of golden-yellow flowers in July; and *G. virgata*, the Madeira Broom, upright to 2–3·7 m (6–12 ft), and short, terminal racemes of yellow flowers in June and July. *G. cinerea*, south-west Europe, grows about 1–2·8 m (3–9 ft), with yellow flowers from July to September. The Spanish Gorse, *G. hispanica*, makes a neat but spiny shrub of 60–90 cm (24–36 in), with golden-yellow flowers in May and June; the Dyer's Greenweed, *G. tinctoria*, of Britain and Europe, 30–90 cm (1–3 ft), is best in its double var *flore pleno*, spreading low, with double yellow flowers in June. *G. lydia*, Balkans, 45 cm (18 in) high, is excellent with butter-yellow bloom in June.

Propagate by seeds in early spring, by cuttings in summer.

Halimium
Family CISTACEAE

Halimium ocymoides

The small evergreen shrubs of this genus form a group very closely related to *Helianthemum*, with opposite, entire leaves, but differing in flower structure in that the style is quite short and straight instead of long and curved. Halimiums are native to the Mediterranean region and therefore need sunny, warm positions, and well-drained soils, doing well where there is lime. They may suffer injury in severe winters unless protected.

H. lasianthum formosum, the Sweet Cistin from Portugal, is perhaps the hardiest species, a slow-growing, spreading shrub, 60–90 cm (24–36 in) high, with grey downy stems, small oblong leaves, and golden-yellow flowers, stained chocolate near the base of the petals, two inches across, in June and July. Another fine Portuguese species is *H. ocymoides*, dense and bushy with downy-grey leaves, and panicles of bright-yellow flowers purple-brown at the base of each petal, in June and July, 45–75 cm (18–30 in) tall. *H. umbellatum* grows erect to 45 cm (18 in), with white flowers, yellow-centred, in erect clusters in June.

Propagate by cuttings taken in June but it is better to layer the shoots. Any pruning should be done after flowering.

Witch Hazel

Hamamelis
Family HAMAMELIDACEAE

Hamamelis mollis

The glory of the Witch Hazels, a group of deciduous shrubs, lies in their flowers which appear on the bare twigs in winter and consist of four narrow, ribbon-like petals, out of a four-sepalled calyx, often coloured within. The leaves are alternate and hazel-like and may colour a pleasing yellow in autumn. The plants are hardy, and at their best in well-drained, humus-rich acid loams, and appreciate dressings of peat or leafmould; in sunshine or partial shade.

The Chinese Witch Hazel, *H. mollis*, 2·1–3 m (7–10 ft) tall, is reputed the best, with deep golden-yellow, scented flowers in January and February, and lemon-yellows on var *pallida*. In the Japanese Witch Hazel, *H. japonica*, growth is spreading up to 2·4 m (8 ft), and the flowers have crumpled yellow petals, with purplish calyces; var *arborea*, growing to 6·1 m (20 ft), golden-yellow flowers; *zuccariniana* is similar but the flowers are lemon-yellow. Their hybrid, *H* × *intermedia*, has provided colourful forms in 'Carmine Red', 'Diane', 'Jelena' and 'Moonlight'.

Propagate by seeds, germination taking two years; by grafting on seedlings of *H. virginiana* in March or April. No regular pruning.

Hebe (syn *Veronica*)
Family SCROPHULARIACEAE

Hebe (syn *Veronica*) *hulkeana*

The Shrubby Speedwells, eligible for our gardens, are chiefly native to New Zealand. They are evergreen, with opposite, entire leaves in four distinct rows, and carry axillary or terminal spikes of small, four-parted flowers in the latter half of summer. Many are tender, and those given here welcome a well-drained loam soil, sunny positions and warm maritime or well-sheltered gardens where frosts are unlikely to be troublesome.

For hardiness, the most valuable are *H. brachysiphon*, bushy and rounded to 2 m (6·5 ft), small leaves, hidden by 5 cm (2 in) racemes of white flowers in July; *H.* × *andersonii*, to 1·8 m (5·75 ft), with long spikes of violet flowers in autumn; and *H. hectori*, rigid stout shoots, with scale leaves, to 60 cm (24 in), white or pinkish flowers in July. For floral beauty under mild conditions, *H. hulkeana*, 0·9–2 m (3–6·5 ft), with lavender-blue sprays in May and June; *H. lyallii*, 45 cm (18 in), white and rose flowers in June; *H. pinguifolia pagei*, good ground cover, white flowers from June to August; and *H. speciosa*, 1·2–1·3 m (4–5 ft), and its hybrids with flowers of blues, red, and purples, are all worthy of careful consideration.

Propagate by softwood cuttings from May to July in a propagating case or frame.

Helianthemum
Family CISTACEAE

Helianthemum vulgare

The shrub species are delightful for the front of shrub borders and rock gardens, given full sun. The leaves are small, entire and opposite, and the five-parted flowers, opening flat like single roses, are freely borne in terminal racemes throughout June and July. They are hardy, and do best in well-drained light soils and revel on limestone and chalk.

The common Sun Rose, *H. nummularium* (syn *H. chamaecistus*), of south-east Europe, growing to 15–45 cm (6–18 in) high and spreading to 60 cm (2 ft) or more, has a host of colourful varieties such as 'Ben Heckla', brick red; 'Ben Adler', orange-red; 'Ben Dearg', crimson lake; 'The Bride', white; and 'Wisley Primrose', primrose yellow; also double-flowering sorts such as 'Jubilee', straw yellow; 'Mrs. Earle', red; 'Rose of Leewood', pink; and 'Watland's Red', deep red. *H. alpestre*, southern Europe, is a charming dwarf of 10 cm (4 in), with small yellow flowers. *H. apenninum*, Europe, spreads low, 45 cm (18 in) high, with white flowers; it has a rosy-red var *roseum*.

Propagate by softwood cuttings in June. Prune after flowering.

Hibiscus
Family MALVACEAE

Hibiscus syriacus

This genus may be handsomely represented in the shrub garden by *H. syriacus*, the Bush Mallow or Bush Hollyhock, introduced from India and China late in the sixteenth century. It is hardy, deciduous, and a late-flowering shrub, growing slowly to 2·4 m (8 ft), with upright habit, having greyish bark, alternate, slender-stalked leaves, 7·5–10 cm (3–4 in) long, generally ovate, but three-lobed and coarsely toothed. The flowers appear singly in the leaf-axils of young shoots, and are hollyhock-like, trumpet-shaped, and up to 10 cm (4 in) across, during autumn. The plants grow readily in most soils and deserve a sunny position, doing best under dry climatic conditions.

There are many varieties, and among the best are: var *coelestis*, single, deep blue flowers; 'Hamabo', single, pale bluish-pink with crimson centre, late flowers; 'Snowdrift', single, white; and 'Woodbridge', which has very large, single flowers of a rich rose-pink, blotched maroon in the centre.

Propagate by cuttings taken with a heel, under a handlight, in July. No regular pruning needed, but may be spurred, by shortening lateral shoots after flowering.

Sea Buckthorn

Hippophae
Family ELAEAGNACEAE

Hippophae rhamnoides

The two species of this genus make tall deciduous shrubs or trees, with branching habit, the shoots often spine-tipped, and alternate, linear leaves, 7·5 cm (3 in) long, dark green above, silvery below, and small, rather insignificant flowers in axillary clusters, on the old wood in April. The plants are dioecious, and to secure the clusters of brilliant orange-yellow berries, at least one male plant should be set among six to eight females. The plants are hardy, and will grow in any ordinary soil, and are especially useful in maritime districts for windbreaks.

H. rhamnoides, the Sea Buckthorn, will grow up to 12 m (40 ft), but can be kept within bounds by pruning. The silvery-grey young shoots and linear leaves are attractive, but the real beauty of the shrub lies in the small, round, shiny, orange-yellow fruits which cluster the branches in autumn, and, being disliked by birds, persist well into the winter. The shrub is a native of temperate Europe and Asia. *H. salicifolia*, comes from the Himalaya with pale yellow fruits, less freely produced.

Propagate female plants by layering in May; for hedges, plants can be raised from seeds in spring. No regular pruning required.

Hydrangea
Family SAXIFRAGACEAE

Hydrangea macrophylla var 'Europa'

This group of shrubs is supreme for midsummer to autumn floral colour; deciduous, with leaves opposite, and flowers in terminal panicles or clusters, the outer flowers often bracted and sterile. They are hardy, and thrive in any good, well-drained, humus-rich loam, pink flowering on soils containing lime, blue on acid. The addition of aluminium sulphate fosters blueness. They grow best in partial shade and deserve shelter.

H. macrophylla the Mophead, from Japan, 1·2–2·4 m (4–8 ft), has many forms—white: 'Mme. E. Mouillière'; pink: 'Parsifal', 'Europa', and 'Hamburg'; red: 'Westfalen', 'Maréchal Foch', and 'Vulcain'; and blue (from pink): 'Vicomtesse de Vibraye', 'Kluis superba', and 'Altona'. 'Lanarth White', 'Blue Wave' and *lilacina* are 'Lacecap' varieties, with large flowers surrounding scented small ones. Of other species, *H. paniculata* var *grandiflora*, 0·9–2·8 m (3–9 ft), Japan, with pointed panicles of white turning pink flowers; *H. serrata*, 1·2 m (4 ft), from Japan, with white, blue and pink varieties, and *H. villosa*, 2·4 m (8 ft), China, blue-flowered, are worth planting.

Propagate by internodal cuttings of leafy shoots in July and August. Prune and thin in February, but spare shoots with terminal buds.

St. John's Wort

Hypericum
Family GUTTIFERAE

Hypericum calycinum

This large genus provides many shrubs notable for their long and generous show of beautiful, five-petalled, stamen-bristling yellow flowers from spring till autumn. The leaves grow opposite or in whorls, marked with transparent glands. The species noted here are hardy, easily cultivated in any reasonably good, well-drained loam and in sunny positions.

One of the hardiest is *H. calycinum*, the 'Rose of Sharon' from the Orient, 30 cm (12 in) high, but spreading vigorously, even under trees, with large lemon-yellow flowers, June to September. Growing upright to 1·2 m (4 ft) or more, 'Rowallane Hybrid' (*H. hookerianum rogersii* × *H. leschenaultii*) is large flowering. *H. patulum*, an evergreen from China, growing to 0·9 m (3 ft), with bushy habit, is best represented by var 'Hidcote' with the largest of flowers.

A good dwarf of 30–45 cm (12–18 in), is *H.* × *moserianum* (*H.* × *calycinum* × *H. patulum*), with ovate, grey-green leaves, and dense terminal clusters of small yellow flowers; its var *tricolor* has flowers marked with white edged with red.

Propagate by cuttings in June, by rooted runners, by seeds in early spring. Prune, if desired, in February.

Ilex
Family AQUIFOLIACEAE

Ilex aquifolium

The hardy hollies give us beauty in foliage and fruit. The leaves are alternate, often toothed but may be entire. The flowers are small, whitish, appearing in spring or early summer. As the plants are unisexual, only females berry. They do well in any good well-drained loam, in sun or shade, and stand up to wind quite well.

I. aquifolium is the evergreen, common Holly of Britain, Europe and Asia, making a large shrub to 6 m (20 ft), with glossy green, spiny-toothed leaves, and bright red berries on the female form in autumn and winter. Of the varieties, fine males for foliage are 'Silver Queen' and 'Golden Queen'. The best of the female berrying kinds include: *fructu luteo*, yellow-berrying; 'Golden King', golden-bordered leaves; and *pyramidalis*. A mixture of males and females is needed for effective berrying. *I. cornuta*, China, densely evergreen bush to 2·4 m (8 ft), has large oblong, spined leaves, and *I. crenata*, Japan, to 3 m (10 ft), small, lance-shaped leaves; *I. pernyi*, China, to 3 m (10 ft), has distinctive, long-spined foliage and berries freely.

Propagate by seeds, stratified in sand for a year, by cuttings in August under handlight. Prune in April or September.

Indigo

Indigofera
Family LEGUMINOSAE

Indigofera gerardiana

The few hardy species of this group of deciduous, leguminous shrubs are attractive with elegant, alternate, pinnate leaves, and racemes of broom-like, pink or purple flowers, freely produced from the leaf-axils of growing shoots successively through summer and autumn. They do best in open, well-drained loams, and should be given warm, sunny positions.

I. gerardiana, Himalaya, is reasonably hardy, growing 0·9–1·2 m (3–4 ft), with graceful, spreading habit in the open, taller on walls, having light, green-grey foliage made up of pinnate leaves, and flowers of bright purplish-rose in racemes up to 12·7 cm (5 in) long, from June onwards. *I. hebepetala*, also from the Himalaya, grows to 1·2 m (4 ft), with long racemes of rose flowers, with a deep crimson standard. Other attractive kinds from China include *I. pendula*, arching and spreading, with leaves to 25 cm (10 in), from stems reaching 1·3–2·4 m (5–8 ft) tall; and *I. potaninii*, 1·2–2 m (4–6 ft), with flowers of clear pink in racemes of 7·5–12·7 cm (3–5 in).

Propagate by cuttings taken with a heel in June. Prune in February, cutting hard back.

Jasminum
Family OLEACEAE

Jasminum nudiflorum

This is a variable genus of upright, climbing or trailing shrubs with several hardy species that are easily grown in any reasonably good garden loam, such as the fine winter-flowering *J. nudiflorum* from China, its green stems ornamented with scented, yellow flowers, springing singly from axils from November onwards. It is best against a wall, growing 3·7–4·5 m (12–15 ft) high. The Common Jasmine, *J. officinale*, Persia, 3 m (10 ft), is best trained on a wall, where its deciduous, pinnate, opposite leaves, and a terminal cluster of fragrant white flowers, can be best displayed in June to September. *J. beesianum*, China, makes rather tangled rose-pink flowers in ones to threes in June and July; but its hybrid with *J. officinale*, *J.* × *stephanense*, grows to 4·5 m (15 ft). *J. parkeri*, north-west India, 30 cm (12 in), with small, alternate, pinnate leaves, yellow flowers in June and *J. revolutum*, Himalaya, a spreading shrub to 2·4 m (8 ft), with terminal clusters of six to twelve yellow flowers in July and August are well worth planting.

Propagate by cuttings of half-ripened shoots in August. Prune immediately after flowering.

Kalmia
Family Ericaceae

Kalmia latifolia

Anyone who gardens on a lime-free, friable, well-drained, but humus-rich loam and in a mild locality should find room for one of the evergreen shrubs of this group. The leaves are entire, oval or lanceolate and crowded radially at the ends of shoots, but the full beauty lies in the cup-shaped flowers borne in clusters in late spring or early summer, followed by egg-shaped seed capsules. They like sunshine tempered by the open branches of nearby shrubs in the hot summer months.

K. latifolia, the Mountain Laurel or Calico Bush of eastern North America, grows bushy, 1–2·4 m (3–8 ft) tall, with alternate, glossy green, lance-shaped leaves, and large clusters of many saucer-shaped, shell-pink flowers from the wood of the previous year in June and July. Var *myrtifolia* is an excellent low form, 6–9 m (2–3 ft) tall, dense with small-leafed foliage and flowers of a deeper pink. *K. polifolia* (syn *K. glauca*), USA, is dwarf and spreading, with narrow, bright green leaves, and rosy-purple flowers in terminal clusters, in April and May; var *microphylla* is a delightful dwarf of 15 cm (6 in), with pretty rose-lilac flowers.

Propagate by layering in May; by cuttings in August in cold frame or greenhouse.

Kerria
Family ROSACEAE

Kerria japonica var *pleniflora*

The single species that represents this genus has been in cultivation with us for over two hundred years, and is an old, much-admired subject in cottage gardens. It is *K. japonica*, originally from China, a deciduous shrub that throws up erect, slender green shoots to 1·2–1·8 m (4–6 ft), branching into zigzagging, twiggy branchlets with a leaf at each corner. The foliage is freshly green, the alternate leaves being long-pointed, ovate, with heart-shaped base and sharply double-toothed margins. The flowers are a buttercup-yellow, appearing singly at the end of lateral shoots, with a single row of five petals, in April and May. It makes an elegant plant for the border or a wall. Its var *pleniflora*, which grows taller, more erect and more robustly, is a good wall plant, carrying numerous orange-yellow, double, ball-shaped flowers, up to 5 cm (2 in) across, from April to June or longer. Kerrias are easy to grow, doing well in any good, reasonably well-drained garden soil, even chalk, and in sun or partial shade.

Propagate by division in March; by layering in May; by cuttings of young shoots in June and July, under handlights. Prune immediately after flowering, thinning the older wood.

Beauty Bush

Kolkwitzia
Family CAPRIFOLIACEAE

Kolkwitzia amabilis

The genus embraces only one species, a deciduous shrub of considerable charm, *K. amabilis*, sometimes called 'Wilson's Beauty Bush' after E. H. Wilson, who collected it in the Hupeh province of China and introduced it at the beginning of the present century. It is a deciduous shrub of erect habit, growing to 2 m (6·5 ft) tall, with rough or bristly stems, clothed with broad ovate, deeply veined, hairy and short-stalked leaves, distantly toothed and ending in a long, recurving point, growing opposite. The flowers are freely produced in late May and June, bell or funnel-shaped with the mouth five-lobed, and beautifully coloured pink with yellow throat, in corymbs borne at the ends of lateral branchlets. 'Pink Cloud' is a very fine cultivar. The shrubs are hardy, tolerate lime, and grow well in any garden soil which drains readily and contains adequate humus. They do best in a sunny, hot position, with the roots mulched.

Propagate by 5–7·5 cm (2–3 in) long cuttings of the current year's shoots, inserted in a propagating case or frame in June or July. The only pruning needed is an occasional thinning of the stems after flowering.

Lavandula
Family LABIATAE

Lavandula spica

The Lavenders are among the pleasantest small shrubs to grow, with their square young stems lined with opposite, grey-green downy leaves, and long, upright, slender flower-stalks carrying flowers in crowded whirls forming spikes 2·5–7·5 cm (1–3 in) long, and aromatically fragrant in every part. They grow well in any garden soil that is well drained, particularly in sandy loams, and they love full sun.

The Common Old English or Mitcham Lavender, *L. spica*, from the Mediterranean region, grows to about 0·9 m (3 ft) high, with as much spread, with grey downy, linear leaves and spikes of grey-blue, finely-scented flowers in July and August. It has notable varieties in 'Twickle Purple' with long, dark purplish flower-heads; *nana atropurpurea* ('Hidcote' var), dwarf, compact, and 'Folgate' dwarf to 60 cm (2 ft), with lavender-blue flowers. *L. stoechas*, from south-west Europe, grows 0·6–0·9 m (2–3 ft), and is distinctive with purple, bracted flowers, almost bottle-shaped.

Propagate from seeds in spring; by cuttings of unflowered shoots in July to October.

Himalayan Honeysuckle

Leycesteria
Family CAPRIFOLIACEAE

Leycesteria formosa

Of the two species forming this genus, only one can be considered hardy, and even then may be cut down to ground-level in severe winters. It is *L. formosa*, the Himalayan Honeysuckle or Flowering Nutmeg from the Himalaya, a shrub of character that rewards one for making a place for it in the shrub garden.

It is distinctive for its stout, hollow, thin-walled stems of vivid sea-green, with 15 cm (6 in) long, ovate, long pointed, heart-shaped based leaves, slightly toothed and downy-grey beneath, and notable for its flowers which are whitish and funnel-shaped and hang in drooping clusters enclosed by conspicuous, claret-purple bracts, July to September, giving way to reddish-purple fruits, like small gooseberries, to which birds are partial. It normally grows from 1·2–2·4 m (4–8 ft) tall, and a place should be found for it in a slightly shaded corner where the soil is deep loam, rich and well drained. It is a good shrub for wild coverts, where the berries provide food for game-birds.

Propagate by seeds in a cold frame in February; by cuttings of shoots with a heel in autumn, under handlights. Prune, when necessary, in February.

Ligustrum
Family OLEACEAE

Ligustrum sinense

The Privets number over fifty species, and some of them are handsome enough to be grown as specimens. All have opposite, entire, short-stalked leaves, bear small, tubular, white or yellowish flowers in terminal panicles, followed by black or dark-purple berries. They grow quickly, and are easy to cultivate, in ordinary garden soils, in shade or sun.

For hedging or training, *L. ovalifolium* from Japan is best, growing erect up to 4·5 m (15 ft), with glossy evergreen leaves, and its var *aureum*, though less vigorous, is the best golden type, its leaves irregularly margined with yellow. For flowering beauty, *L. quihoui*, a Chinese deciduous shrub, of good rounded habit up to 2·4 m (8 ft), leads in popularity with slender, long panicles of white flowers up to 45 cm (18 in) in August and September. *L. sinense*, China, is a graceful, partially evergreen shrub, growing to 3·7 m (12 ft) high, bearing 7·5–10 cm (3–4 in) panicles of small, white flowers freely in July, fragrant, and followed by dark purple berries.

Propagate by cuttings of shoots taken in August, 15–23 cm (6–9 in) long. Clip hedges in June and September. Specimen shrubs need no regular pruning.

Spice Bush

Lindera
Family LAURACEAE

Lindera benzoin

This is a race of aromatic shrubs, mainly deciduous, the leaves are entire and alternate, turning yellow in autumn, and the flowers small yellowish, and unisexual, appearing in small, axillary clusters before the leaves. They need a lime-free soil, preferably loamy and well drained, and deserve a sheltered, sunny position to be fully rewarding.

L. Benzoin (syn *Benzoin aestivale*) is the Spice Bush of North America, and quite hardy. It makes a shapely rounded shrub of 1·8–3·7 m (6–8 ft), with deciduous, obovate, thin, green leaves, and up to 12·5 cm (5 in) long, which give off a pungent spicy aroma when crushed. The small, greenish-yellow flowers appear in dense small clusters at the joints of the previous year's growth before the leaves unfold, in March and April, and on female plants are followed by small, oblong, reddish berries. *L.* (*Parabenzoin*) *praecox* is deciduous but only hardy for a sheltered, warm wall in a mild district, where it will grow up to 4·5 m (15 ft), with greenish-yellow flowers in March and April, seen against shining brown shoots.

Propagate by cuttings taken in July or August. No regular pruning is needed.

Lithospermum
Family BORAGINACEAE

Lithospermum diffusum

The shrubs of this genus are low growing and evergreen, with alternate narrow leaves, but to be considered indispensable where conditions are favourable.

The best of these dwarfs is *L. diffusum* (syn *L. prostatum*), which comes from southern Europe, and sends out prostrate, slender stems as far as 60 cm (2 ft), with small, linear-oblong, rough bristly, green leaves to form a carpeting mass, rarely more than 30 cm (12 in) high, with leafy terminal spikes of stalkless, funnel-shaped deep blue flowers in May. It has several forms, a most popular finely blue-coloured var 'Heavenly Blue' and var 'Grace Ward' with slightly larger and slightly deeper blue flowers. These plants must have lime-free soil, preferably well drained and loamy. The roots like coolness, but the plants otherwise like sun, and do well over rocks or down walls. *L. oleifolium*, Spain, prostrate growing, with grey-green rounded leaves, white beneath, and large blue flowers in June; and *L. rosmarinifolium*, southern Italy, a rounded bush with narrow leaves and bright blue flowers in January and February, need warm, sheltered sites but do not mind lime in the soil.

Propagate by seeds, or by cuttings in summer.

Lonicera
Family CAPRIFOLIACEAE

Lonicera fragrantissima

The bush or shrubby species of Honeysuckle form a separate section of the genus. They are deciduous or evergreen, with opposite, entire, short-stalked leaves, and with flowers paired on one stalk from the leaf-axils. They do best in a humus-rich soil, free-draining, and in warm, sunny positions, and are quite hardy.

The evergreen *L. nitida*, China, with its small, ovate leaves crowding its dense stems, is much used for quick-growing hedges up to 1·2 m (4 ft), and var *fertilis* is its stiffer form. *L. fragrantissima*, semi-evergreen, stiffish oval, 5 cm (2 in) green leaves, and highly scented, white flowers in winter, growing 1·2–2 m (4–6·5 ft); *L. standishii*, also half-evergreen, 1·8–2·4 m (6–8 ft), with 10 cm (4 in) lanceolate leaves, and creamy-white, fragrant flowers in winter; and their hybrid, *L. × purpusii*, with creamy-white scented winter flowers; *L. syringantha*, 1·8–2·4 m (6–8 ft), with slender spreading stems and small, deciduous, blue-green leaves, and rose-lilac, sweetly scented flowers in May and June. The Pyrenees provides *L. pyrenaica*, dwarf of 0·6–0·9 m (24–34 in), deciduous, grey-green, oval leaves, rose and white flowers in May and June, and later, red berries.

Propagate by cuttings in July and August, by layering in August to November, or by seeds in spring.

Lonicera
Family CAPRIFOLIACEAE

Lonicera sempervirens

The Climbing Honeysuckles are best confined to pergolas, arches, trellis and similar supports at the boundaries of the garden, since if allowed to twine up living trees or shrubs there is a real danger of the growth of the latter being constricted and strangled. They are excellent, however, to clothe old stumps or to range in the wild garden. They do not mind shade, but like a moist, deep soil, reasonably free-draining.

Good deciduous types include *L. periclymenum*, the Woodbine native to Britain and Europe, climbing to 6·1 m (20 ft), with green, ovate leaves, and its sweetly scented, yellow-white, flushed red, tubular flowers in clusters from May to September; its best varieties being *belgica*, the early Dutch Honeysuckle, with flowers deeply tinged purplish-red, and *serotina*, the late form, with flowers dark purple outside; all bearing red berries later. *L. tragophylla*, China, 3–3·7 m (10–12 ft), is most attractive, with coppery leaves, and large clusters of big orange-red flowers from June. *L. sempervirens*, USA, 6·1 m (20 ft), orange, yellow and red flowers is semi-evergreen and only hardy enough for the south-west.

Propagate by cuttings in July or August or by layering.

Magnolia
Family MAGNOLIACEAE

Magnolia stellata

A genus of magnificent shrubs and trees. With their large, firm, entire, alternate leaves and large, strikingly beautiful solitary flowers, they are aristocrats of the garden, and their culture is not difficult given good, humus-rich, well-drained deep loam and a sunny position, sheltered to the north and east.

M. stellata, Japan, grows slowly from 1·2–4·5 m (5–15 ft), with white, semi-double flowers made up of narrow petals, in March and April, and has a var *rosea*, pink-flowered. *M. denudata* (syn *M. conspicua*) is the Yulan of China, making a large shrub to 6·1 m (20 ft) in time, with white, 12·7 cm (5 in) cup-shaped flowers in March and May, and long, oval leaves. *M.* × *soulangeana*, (*M. denudata* × *M. liliflora*) is grown as a tall spreading shrub, to 6·1 m (20 ft) high, having goblet-like, white, flushed purple, flowers in April, and var *alba superba*, white, rosy-purple outside. Of those flowering when in leaf, *M. sieboldii*, Japan 4·5 m (15 ft), scented, white cups in May; *M. wilsonii*, China, to 6·1 m (20 ft), with pendent, white flowers in June; and the evergreens *M. grandiflora*, USA, var 'Exmouth', to 4·5 m (15 ft) and *M. delavayi*, to 9 m (30 ft) of Yunnan, are best.

Propagate by layering in July to October.

Mahonia
Family BERBERIDACEAE

Mahonia aquifolium

The Mahonias are related to *Berberis*, but differ in having compound pinnate leaves, which are alternate and evergreen, and stems without spines. The flowers are usually yellow, and are carried in erect, spike-like racemes from the ends of shoots, yielding place to bluish-black berries. They thrive in any good garden soil, including one of lime content, in sun or some shade.

M. aquifolium, the Oregon Grape from North America, grows 0·6–0·9 m (2–3 ft) tall, with glossy green pinnate leaves made up of spiny leaflets, and rich yellow flowers in clusters of racemes, February to April. *M. bealei* and *M. japonica* are often confused, but the former comes from China, growing to 2 m (6·5 ft) with upright, 7·5–15 cm (3–6 in) racemes of yellow flowers during winter; and the latter comes from Japan, grows 2·8 m (8 ft) or more and has drooping racemes of fragrant, lemon-yellow flowers, and fine pinnate foliage. Perhaps the most striking species is *M. lomariifolia*, Yunnan, 2 m (6·5 ft), with leaves having up to nineteen pairs of blue-green leaflets. It needs warm shelter.

Propagate by layering in spring and by cuttings in summer. Prune after flowering.

Myrtle

Myrtus
Family MYRTACEAE

Myrtus communis

From this genus of evergreen shrubs come pleasantly-scented plants for the shrub border. The leaves are usually opposite, short stalked, and entire; the flowers are white and solitary from the leaf-axils and the fruits roundish berries, often edible. As they are from warm regions, they need well-sheltered positions and are best grown against walls, except in the south-west, and succeed in any good, reasonably well-drained loam.

The Common Myrtle, *M. communis*, from the Mediterranean region, makes a well-leafed shrub, 2·4–3 m (8–10 ft) high, with shining deep green, scented ovate leaves, creamy-white flowers with many stamens in July, followed by purple-black berries; var *tarentina* has smaller leaves and whitish fruits; and var *variegata*, variegated cream and green leaves. A Chilean Myrtle, *M. apiculata* (syn *luma*), becomes a fine large shrub of 6–8 m (18–24 ft) in mild gardens, the stems a downy reddish-cinnamon brown; the leaves small and decorative, oval and dark green; the flowers white and scented in summer, followed by sweet black fruits.

Propagate by cuttings under handlights in July. No regular pruning, but shaping may be done in March.

Neillia
Family ROSACEAE

Neillia longiracemosa

The shrubs of this group are all deciduous species native to China and the Himalayan region, and closely resemble the related shrubs of *Spiraea* in habit. The leaves are alternate, ovate, double-toothed and lobed as a rule, and the flowers are five-parted and small in many-flowered racemes, followed by dry capsules, containing shining dark seeds. The plants are hardy and easily grown in any fair garden loam holding moisture, and they like a sunny open position.

The best species is *N. longiracemosa* of western China, with slender stems, to 2 m (6·5 ft) tall, somewhat downy, green tri-lobed, slender-pointed and double-toothed leaves, 5–10 cm (2–4 in) long, and drooping racemes of rosy-pink flowers from the ends of shoots in May and June. *N. sinensis*, central China, grows 1·2–2 m (4–6·5 ft), with smooth brown stems, and smaller ovate leaves, and white flowers in small racemes in May and June; and *N. thibetica*, Tibet, is similar, but with downy shoots, somewhat larger leaves, and more floriferous with dense, longer, terminal sprays of flowers.

Propagate by seeds under glass, by half-ripened cuttings in July or August.

Daisy Bush

Olearia
Family COMPOSITAE

Olearia × haastii

The Daisy Bushes or Tree Daises comprise a genus of over a hundred evergreen shrubs and trees, native to Australasia, but many are of doubtful hardiness. Their attractive foliage of alternate (opposite in a few species) leathery green leaves, white or buff beneath, heads of Daisy-like flowers, and good habit make them desirable plants, especially for seaside planting since they stand up well to wind. They are equally happy in limy or lime-free soils, given good drainage, full sunshine, and shelter from the east and north, or a sunny wall.

The hardiest is the hybrid *O. × haastii*, New Zealand, a round bush up to 1·3 m (5 ft), with entire ovate leaves, white beneath, and covered with scented clusters of small white flowers in July and August. *O. albida*, a shrub of about 3 m (10 ft), with polished dark green, ovate leaves, much white-felted beneath, and white flowers, July and August; and *O. nummularifolia*, 1·2–2 m (4–6·5 ft), with small, yellowish-green leaves, and white flowers, in June and July, are fairly hardy. *O. macrodonta*, 3–3·7 m (10–12 ft), greyish, holly-like leaves, scented white flowers in June, is one of the best.

Propagate by cuttings in July or August under handlights.

Osmanthus
Family OLEACEAE

Osmanthus delavayi

This is a small genus of evergreen shrubs with attractive foliage of dark green, shiny, spine-toothed, holly-like, opposite leaves, delightfully scented, white tubular, four-lobed, Jasmine-like small flowers in axillary clusters, which may be succeeded by blue-purple, one-seeded fruits. They are generally hardy, thriving in ordinary garden loams, and welcoming warm, sunny positions with shelter from the worst severities of our winters.

The most rewarding species is *O. delavayi* (syn *Siphonosmanthus delavayi*), a shrub of spreading, arching habit of 2 m (6·5 ft) or more, with small, ovate, sharply-toothed, glossy green leaves, and clusters of small very fragrant, pure white flowers from the leaf-axils in May and April, succeeded by blue-black berries. *O. heterophyllus* (syn *O. ilicifolius*), Japan, is a compact, holly-like shrub of 3 m (10 ft), with its scented flowers opening in autumn, and has var *aureo-variegatus*, with yellow-margined leaves. *O. armatus*, China, is handsome, to 4·5 m (15 ft), with spined, leathery, leaves and creamy-white flowers in September.

Propagate by cuttings taken in July or August. No regular pruning is required, but training or shaping can be done in May.

Mountain Spurge

Pachysandra
Family BUXACEAE

Pachysandra terminalis

The species of this group are low growing evergreen, semi-woody shrubs, chiefly valuable for carpeting under trees and growing in densely shaded places where little else will. The stems are fleshy, with alternate leaves, crowded in whorl-like groups at the ends. The flowers are small and unisexual, without petals, and produced in spikes. They are hardy and thrive in ordinary loams.

P. terminalis is the Mountain Spurge from Japan, with stems less than 30 cm (12 in) high, but spreading by means of creeping root-stocks to 1 m (3 ft) or so. The leaves are roughly diamond-shaped, with three prominent veins to the base, coarsely toothed to the apex and 5–7·5 cm (2–3 in) long. In April, small 5 cm (2 in) spikes of greenish-white flowers, tinged purplish, are produced at the end of the shoots, followed by capsule-fruits with three horns from persisting styles. *P. procumbens*, the Alleghany Spurge of south-east United States, is similar, but with larger leaves and shoots which are downy, and 10–12·5 cm (4–5 in) spikes of white or pinkish flowers in April.

Propagate by division in spring; by cuttings in June. No regular pruning needed.

Paeonia
Family RANUNCULACEAE

Paeonia suffruticosa

The 'Tree' Paeonies are really shrubby species of this genus of perennial herbs, and provide glorious colour for the shrub garden. They need a deep well-cultivated, rich loam, regularly mulched, and do best in sheltered positions, but with warm sun in summer. They are hardy but start into growth early, and should be protected against spring frosts.

P. delavayi makes a handsome shrub up to 1·3 m (5 ft), with deep red flowers and a centre of yellow anthers in May. *P. lutea* of China and Tibet grows up to 1·3 m (5 ft), with bi-ternate leaves, and yellow flowers up to 10 cm (4 in) across, and its var *ludlowii* has even larger flowers, in June. *P. suffruticosa* (syn *P. moutan*) of China and Tibet is the Moutan Paeony, growing to 1·3 m (5 ft), with rather rigid, brittle and hard branching two-pinnate leaves, and rose-pink flowers in May, and has many single and double coloured forms, ranging from white to crimson. Crossing *P. lutea* × *P. suffruticosa* has given fine yellow hybrids in bright yellow, 'Chromatella' and 'Souvenir de Maxime Cornu', scented, very big, bright yellow with carmine edges. Other notable hybrids are to be found in growers' list.

Propagate by layering in early spring.

Passiflora
Family PASSIFLORACEAE

Passiflora caerulea

Out of over three hundred species of climbing plants of this genus, only one is of sufficient hardiness to be grown out of doors, and only in the south and west or on a well-sheltered, sunny south wall. Any good garden loam will suit, enriched with humus-forming material.

The species is *P. caerulea*, the Blue Passion Flower of Brazil and central South America. It is a vigorous climber, growing to 6 m (20 ft), by tendrils, and having nominally evergreen alternate leaves, of five to seven lobes, palmately arranged. From June to September the flowers rise singly from the leaf-axils, exotic in construction and colouring. The tubular calyx opens to five greenish-white sepals, the same number of white or pinkish petals, and rings of thread-like filaments, purple based, then white and blue, making the corona; from the centre rises the gynophore or stem carrying the five stamens, the ovary, and the three styles at the top. There is a var 'Constance Elliott' with large, ivory-white flowers.

Propagate by seeds in February under glass; by cuttings in July. Prune in February or March, cutting shoots back by one-half their length.

Pernettya
Family ERICACEAE

Pernettya mucronata

The charm of these low-growing evergreen shrubs lies partly in their alternate, short-stalked, firm, leathery, ovate and serrated leaves, partly in their five-parted, small flowers like those of Lily-of-the-Valley, but mostly in their ornamental berry fruits, freely borne in autumn. Like so many members of the Erica family, they need a lime-free soil and rejoice in peat. The flowers are pseudo-hermaphrodite and self-sterile, and it is wise to plant a male plant or two with the females to ensure good berrying displays.

P. mucronata from the Magellan area of South America is hardy. It makes a stiff, bushy shrub, 0·6–1·3 m (2–5 ft) tall, densely packed with small, dark green, pointed, oval leaves, and bearing small, white flowers from the leaf-axils on wood of the previous year in May and June, which give way to masses of white, pink, reddish or purple berries. Of many varieties 'Bell's Seedling' stands out with larger leaves and bigger, scarlet berries; *alba* has white berries; *rosea*, rose-pink; *mascula*, purplish-pink; and there are others. Other species are only hardy for the mildest counties.

Propagate by layering in spring; by cuttings in August; or detach rooted offsets.

Mock Orange

Philadelphus
Family PHILADELPHACEAE

Philadelphus × lemoinei
var 'Bouquet Blanc'

The Mock Oranges, mis-called 'Syringa', are a group of some forty deciduous shrubs with solid pithed stems, opposite, usually ovate and widely toothed leaves, and white, four-parted flowers, often orange-scented. Invaluable for floral beauty in June and July, but without much grace in habit, their hardiness and willingness to thrive in poorish soils, limy or not, are assets.

Outstanding hybrids, such as *P. × lemoinei*, are erect in growth to 1·8 m (6 ft), with highly-scented white flowers, having good single forms in 'Avalanche', and double in 'Virginale', 'Bouquet Blanc' and 'Manteau d'Hermine'. *P. × purpureo-maculatus*, 1·8 m (6 ft), has purple blotching at the base of its flowers; and in its vars 'Belle Etoile', and 'Sybille'. Of the species, *P. coronarius*, Asia Minor, grows to 3·7 m (12 ft), with creamy-white, scented racemes, and a golden-leaved form in var *aureus*. The Chinese *P. delavayi*, to 3 m (10 ft) and *P. incanus*, 1·8 m (6 ft), bear racemes of scented flowers.

Propagate by cuttings in July. Prune immediately after flowering, removing branches that have flowered.

Pieris
Family Ericaceae

Pieris japonica

These evergreen shrubs with alternate, finely toothed leaves are valuable for their white, waxy, urn-shaped flowers borne early in spring in terminal panicles. They thrive in lime-free, humus-rich soils, but since they flower in March and April, they should be given frost-free sites, sheltered from drying east winds.

One of the best is *P. formosa*, China, 1·8–2·8 m (6–9 ft) tall, with long lanceolate, minutely toothed, glossy green leaves, and stiff spikes of nodding, green-sepaled, white flowers, like those of Lily-of-the-Valley in shape and scent, in May; var *forrestii*, 1·8–3·7 m (6–12 ft), is pink and red in foliage when the leaves are young, and has rather larger flowers; both spread widely by suckers. Japan provides *P. japonica*, a branching shrub to 3 m (10 ft), with brown branchlets, oblanceolate, pointed leaves, and the white flowers in drooping terminal racemes in March and April; with var *variegata*, having leaves with yellowish margins; and *P. taiwanensis*, Formosa, erect and rounded to 3 m (10 ft), with brightly coloured young foliage, and erect sprays of flowers in April.

Propagate by seeds under glass in March; by heeled cuttings in August; by layering in autumn.

Pittosporum
Family PITTOSPORACEAE

Pittosporum tobira

The evergreen shrubs of this genus are chiefly valuable for their beautiful foliage and blossom fragrance. The leaves are alternate, in whorls towards the ends of branches, and fleshy with a network of green and white veins. The flowers are generally scented. Being tender, the plants succeed in the open only in mild districts; elsewhere they need the shelter of a wall or cold greenhouse. Any good garden loam is suitable.

Among the hardiest are *P. dallii*, New Zealand, a rounded shrub to 5·4 m (18 ft), with toothed to entire, dull green, elliptical leaves, and white, scented flowers in June; and *P. tenuifolium*, New Zealand, a tall shrub to 6·1 m (20 ft) or more, with wavy-edged, pale shining green, leaves, on blackish shoots, and honey-scented, dark purplish flowers, in May; and its vars. Others for the milder gardens include: *P. eugenioides* var *variegatum*, New Zealand, 3·7–6·1 m (12–20 ft), prettily foliaged, yellow-flowering; and *P. tobira*, a bushy shrub of 3–6·1 m (10–20 ft), from China and Japan, with fine creamy, scented flowers in summer.

Propagate by cuttings taken in autumn in a cold frame. No regular pruning needed.

Polygonum
Family POLYGONACEAE

Polygonum baldschuanicum

The genus embraces annuals, perennials, sub-shrubs and climbing shrubs to over 150 species. It is the last which are useful in the shrub garden.

Polygonum baldschuanicum from south Turkestan or Bokhara is a handsome, quick-growing, deciduous climbing shrub, its slender woody stems reaching 6·1–12·2 m (20–40 ft) high, and with its foliage of large, alternate, heart-shaped, blunt- or sharp-pointed, pale green leaves, and feathery panicles of small, white or pinkish-white flowers freely produced from the leaf-axils and the ends of shoots from July to Autumn, it is first class for ramping over old trees or unsightly objects where it can be spread with freedom. It can be grown with striking effect up a wire to the overhead branches of established trees such as Beech, or up fence wire-netting to shut out an unsightly view. *P. aubertii*, China, is similar in habit but with clear white flowers in somewhat smaller panicles, which may not appear until August. These climbing shrubs do excellently in any ordinary garden soil.

Propagate by cuttings, taking them with a heel, in July or August. Prune in spring, if needed.

Shrubby Cinquefoil

Potentilla
Family ROSACEAE

Potentilla fruticosa

The majority of the species in this group of some 350 members are herbaceous plants. The shrub forms, however, are to be valued for their easy growth and free flowering through summer into autumn. The leaves are alternate and pinnate, and the strawberry-like flowers, with rounded petals, appear solitary or few in number at the ends of branches. The Shrubby Cinquefoils are hardy, and ready to grow on almost any soil, given good drainage, and may be placed in sunshine or partial shade.

The species *P. fruticosa* is a deciduous upright shrub to 1·2 m (4 ft) or so, with shreddy barked branching stems, pinnate leaves made up of five or seven 2·5 cm (1 in), pointed, lanceolate leaflets, and five-petalled, yellow flowers, produced in ones to threes over a long period from June to September. The plant is native to the northern hemisphere, including Britain, and there are now many garden varieties, such as 'Cornish Cream', white; 'Katherine Dykes', primrose yellow; 'Red Ace', vermilion; 'Tangerine', orange; and *vilmoriniana*, cream, silvery leaves. *P. arbuscula*, 0·9 m (3 ft) tall, clear yellow, Himalaya, is good.

Propagate by cuttings taken with a heel in late summer. Prune flowered shoots in March.

Prunus
Family ROSACEAE

Prunus laurocerasus

The Laurel section of *Prunus* differs from the others in that the species are evergreen and bear their flowers in long racemes. The Common or Cherry Laurel, *P. laurocerasus*, came from Eastern Europe and Asia Minor and makes a quick-growing shrub to a height of 6·1 m (20 ft) if unchecked, with oblong, lanceolate, glossy dark green, leathery leaves, to 15 cm (6 in) long, and small white flowers in short, erect racemes from leaf-axils in April, giving way to purple-black, egg-shaped fruits. It has several forms, notably *rotundifolia*, of bushy habit, well suited for hedges; *schipkaensis*, with smaller leaves and low growing; and *zabeliana*, suited to banks. *P. lusitanica*, the Portugal Laurel, from the Iberian peninsula, is a fine evergreen reaching to 6·1 m (20 ft) tall, with ovate, dark glossy-green, finely toothed and red-stalked leaves, and racemes of hawthorn-scented white flowers, up to 25 cm (10 in) long in June, followed by dark purple fruits.

Propagation of *Prunus* may be attempted by cuttings of firm shoots in July or August; species by seeds. Varieties are often grafted or budded on seedlings of their kind or of related species. Any pruning to shape should be done in summer.

Firethorn

Pyracantha
Family ROSACEAE

Pyracantha coccinea var *lalandei*

The Firethorns form a group of evergreen shrubs with spiny branches. The leaves are alternate or in clusters, the flowers always white and small in branched clusters, and followed by small colourful berries or pomes, freely borne in autumn. All species are hardy, and thrive in any reasonably well-drained soil.

P. coccinea is the Firethorn, native to southern Europe, making a tall shrub or small tree of up to 4·5 m (15 ft), with small, narrowly oval leaves, white flowers in June, with clusters of bright coral-red berries in autumn; its var *lalandei* is outstanding, more vigorous and with brilliant orange-red fruits. *P. rogersiana*, China, is of dense bushy habit to 3 m (10 ft) tall, with bright green, oblanceolate leaves, hawthorn-white flowers in June, and orange berries in autumn; var *flava* has bright yellow fruits. *P. atalantioides* is upright growing to 4·8 m (16 ft), with scarlet berries, and var *aurea* is yellow-fruiting. A notable hybrid, × *watereri*, is red-fruiting.

Propagate by heeled cuttings in July or August; by seeds sown under glass in February. No regular pruning for bushes. On walls, lateral shoots can be spurred or cut back in autumn.

Ribes
Family GROSSULARIACEAE

Ribes sanguineum

The genus includes Gooseberries as well as Currants. In Currants the stems are spineless, the flower-stalks unjointed; in Gooseberries, stems are spiny and flower stalks jointed. Both have alternate leaves, lobed and toothed, and small flowers, usually followed by juicy fruits. They are easily grown in any moderate garden loam, in sun or semi-shade.

Of the Currants, *R. odoratum*, western North America, is the Golden Currant, lax in habit to 2·4 m (8 ft), with bright yellow, tubular, scented flowers in drooping racemes in April, then black fruits. *R. sanguineum* is the Flowering Currant from western North America, a branching shrub of 1·8–2·8 m (6–9 ft), unfailing with its racemes of deep-rosy flowers in April, and soft green, lobed and heart-shaped, downy leaves. Vars are 'Pulborough Scarlet', deep red; 'King Edward VII', deep crimson flowers; and *splendens*, almost blood-red flowers. Of the Gooseberries, *R. speciosum*, California, grows 2·1–3 m (6–10 ft), with bristly shoots, and bright red, slender flowers, drooping, fuchsia-like, in clusters in April.

Propagate by cuttings taken from July to October. May be pruned by cutting back flowered shoots, late spring.

Rose

Rosa
Family ROSACEAE

Rosa banksiae

This genus of deciduous shrubs has over 120 species, and thousands of hybrid and varietal forms; having thorny stems, alternate, pinnate, stipulate leaves, five-parted flowers and fleshy seed receptacles or hips. They grow in most soils, given good drainage and humus, and open sun.

Species of bushy habit for flowering June to September, include: *R. centifolia*, the Cabbage or Provence Rose, with double, scented pink flowers, and its var *mucosa*, the Moss Rose; *R. damascena*, the Damask Rose of Asia Minor, with pink to red, double scented flowers; and its var *versicolor*, the York and Lancaster Rose. China gives us *R. chinensis*, the China or Monthly Rose, parent of many varieties; *R. hugonis*, 1·8–2·8 m (6–9 ft), yellow-flowering, but better in the hybrid *R.* × *cantabrigiensis*; *R. moyesii*, 1·8–3 m (6–10 ft), blood-red flowers and vermillion hips; *R. rugosa*, the Ramanas Rose, 1·2–2·4 m (5–8 ft), rosy-red flowers, and roundish, orange-red hips; and *R. farreri*, 1·2–2·4 m (5–8 ft), pale pink and its var *persetosa*, the Threepenny-bit Rose. *R. moschata*, the Musk Rose, Himalaya, has many bush forms of beauty. *R. banksiae*, the Banksian Rose, China, and its varieties like a sunny wall, flowering white or yellow in May and June.

Rosa
Family ROSACEAE

Rosa (Hybrid Perpetual)
'Mrs. John Laing'

The Hybrid Perpetual Rose, so popular in Victorian days, originated in France, from chance crossings and selection between *R. centifolia*, *R. damascena*, *R. gallica*, their varieties, and hybrids of *R. chinensis*. They flower in summer and sometimes into autumn, with double flowers, well perfumed and opening flattish, and are hardy. They can be grown in ordinary garden soils without trouble.

The outstanding variety is 'Frau Karl Druschki', with large blooms of purest white, shell-like petals, freely produced from June to September, growing to 1·8 m (6 ft). 'Hugh Dickson' produces long stems which may be pegged down to bloom along their length, bearing large, full flowers, intense crimson, shaded red, and sweetly scented. Others are 'General Jacqueminot', geranium-red, shaded strawberry-red flowers; 'Mrs. John Laing', bearing beautiful soft pink, scented flowers; and 'Ulrich Brunner', cerise-red, large blooms. All make robust bushes up to 1·8 m (6 ft), requiring little pruning beyond removal of dead twigs and shortening of weak growth. The crossing of Hybrid Perpetuals with *R. eglanteria* has yielded the Penzance Briers, vigorous shrubs growing 1·8–3 m (6–10 ft), with semi-double, fragrant flowers.

Tea Rose: China Rose

Rosa
Family ROSACEAE

Rosa (*Tea*) 'Lady Hillingdon'

Tea Roses were so called because their scent was comparable to that of a delicate China tea. They were derived from *R. odorata*, a species long cultivated in China, making a bush or climber 1·8–3·7 m (6–12 ft), having semi-evergreen leaves, and large; fragrant, semi-double or double flowers. Developed in France, many varieties prove too tender for outdoor cultivation in Britain. Those worth planting for the perfect shapeliness of their flowers, their exquisite scent and the delicate tints are 'Lady Hillingdon' for a sheltered corner out of doors, bearing long-pointed buds which open to flowers of deep apricot yellow, seen against dark green foliage; 'Devoniensis', a good bush with flowers of pale cream, tinged blush-pink in the centre; and 'Gloire de Dijon', generally grown on walls as a climbing shrub, with flowers chamois-yellow, shaded orange in the centre.

The crossing of *R. chinensis* and its dwarf var *semperflorens*, has yielded the China or Monthly Roses and hybrids, of which 'Cecile Brunner', sprays of pink scented flowers; 'Fellemberg', rose-carmine clustered flowers; 'Little White Pet', double white flowers; and 'Perle d'Or', orange-yellow blooms, are choice.

Rosa
Family ROSACEAE

Rosa (*Hybrid Tea*) 'Mrs Sam McGredy'

Hybrid Tea Roses, largely from crosses of Hybrid Perpetuals and Tea Roses, now make up a new class called the 'Large Flowered Bush' roses. They are hardy, free-flowering, bearing semi-double or double flowers in a wide range of colours, more or less scented, and are recurrent-flowering bushes of moderate height.

Varieties are legion, and only a nucleus selection is attempted here, according to flower colour: white—'Message', 'Pascali', 'Virgo'; light pink—'Ophelia', 'Polly'; medium pink—'Grace de Monaco', 'Lady Sylvia', 'Monique'; deep pink—'Eden Rose', 'Prima Ballerina'; carmine, cerise—'Betty Uprichard', 'Wendy Cussons'; yellow—'Grandpa Dickson', 'Landora', 'Lydia', 'Peace'; orange—'Mrs Sam McGredy', 'Bettina', 'King's Ransom', 'Mojave'; red— 'Alec's Red', 'Ena Harkness', 'Fragrant Cloud', 'Josephine Bruce', 'Uncle Walter'; bicolours—'Chicago Peace', 'Harry Wheatcroft', 'Piccadilly', 'Vienna Charm', 'Rose Gaujard'.

Many of these roses have sported climbing forms; and many can be grown as Standards, grafted on stems of *R. rugosa*.

Propagate by budding in July; by grafting in spring; by cuttings in November. Prune late March or April.

Pernetiana Rose

Rosa
Family ROSACEAE

Rosa (*Pernetiana*)
'Madame Edouard Herriot'

The use of a Rose known as the Persian Yellow, *R. foetida* var *persiana*, native to northern Persia and adjacent lands, as a parent plant with Hybrid Tea Roses introduced yellow colouring into the lines of breeding. This resulted in a class of Roses being developed early in the present century known as Pernetiana, later merged with the Hybrid Teas in the 'Large Flowered Bush' class. Nevertheless, this is the primary source of all the yellow and yellow-orange Hybrid Tea Roses, and a few persist in modern rose growing.

The original crosses are difficult to obtain, but 'Julien Potin', golden-yellow, is still offered. 'Angele Pernet', a vivid orange-yellow, shaded apricot, and lightly scented, holds its place, but the line of breeding is best commemorated in 'Madame Edouard Herriot', also known as 'Daily Mail', with its flowers of bright coral red, shaded yellow and scarlet, and highly fragrant. 'Isobel' is a single rose of carmine, flushed orange-red, and 'Mrs Oakely Fisher', rich orange-yellow, is also single. The Pernetiana Roses are hardy and in cultural requirements and propagation similar to the Hybrid Teas.

Rosa
Family ROSACEAE

Rosa (*Polyantha*) 'Little Dorrit'

For hedges, massing, or freely blooming bushes in the shrub garden, the cluster-flowering classes of Polyantha and Hybrid Polyantha or Floribunda Roses are ideal. Hardy, of compact growth, they produce their flowers freely from summer until autumn.

The Dwarf Polyantha Roses originated in crosses between the small-flowered, clustering *R. multiflora* of Korea and Japan, and the free-blooming *R. chinensis* of China, and a tea-scented variety, apparently unknown. They grow about 45–60 cm (18–24 in) high. A short selection of varieties is 'Baby Faurax', violet blue; 'Coral Cluster', coral pink; 'Ellen Poulsen', deep pink; 'Little Dorrit', coral pink, scented; and 'Paul Crampel', geranium red.

The Floribundas, now classed as the 'Cluster Flowered Bush' group, are from crosses of Polyanthas with Hybrid Tea Roses. Outstanding kinds are 'Anne Poulsen', rose madder; 'Chinatown', yellow; 'Elizabeth of Glamis', pink; 'Evelyn Fison', red; 'Iceberg', white; 'Fashion', salmon pink; 'Karen Poulsen', single, scarlet; 'Frensham', crimson.

For bedding, they are pruned hard in spring; for growth as bushes, little pruning beyond thinning is needed.

Climbing Rose

Rosa
Family ROSACEAE

Rosa (*wichuraiana*) 'Albertine'

Climbing roses are usually divided into two classes, Ramblers, and Climbing, Pillar Roses.

The ramblers are derived from *R. wichuraiana* crossed with other garden Roses, make long shoot growth each year, and remain semi-evergreen. Noteworthy varieties are 'Albertine', scented double flowers of coppery-pink; 'Chaplin's Pink', semi-double, pink; 'Easlea's Golden', yellow streaked crimson; 'Emily Gray', golden-yellow; 'New Dawn', soft pink; and 'Thelma', coral pink, scented. Pruning consists of shortening lateral shoots on the main stems to about three buds in autumn, and occasional on the main stems, more than three years old. The Polyantha Ramblers bear flowers in clusters, and include 'American Pillar', single pink; and 'Phyllis Bide', pale gold, shaded carmine.

The Climbing and Pillar Roses may be sports of Tea Roses, of Hybrid teas, or of Pernetianas. 'Mme Gregoire Straechelin', pink, 'Zephirine Drouhin', clear pink, and 'William Allen Richardson', orange-yellow, are good.

Pruning should be light in this group, chiefly removal of dead wood and a light trimming or thinning in Autumn.

Rosmarinus
Family LABIATAE

Rosmarinus officinalis

The number of species in this genus is botanically in dispute, but the species and its varieties grown out of doors in Britain is *R. officinalis*, native to southern Europe and Asia Minor, but cultivated in Britain for five centuries or more. It is an evergreen shrub, of loose habit and attaining to about 2 m (6 ft) high, and as wide, if left to grow naturally. With pruning, however, it can be hedge-like. With opposite, linear, blunt-ended leaves, up to 5 cm (2 in) long, dark green above, white-felted beneath, and having recurved margins, on downy shoots it is attractive at all seasons, and the strong aromatic fragrance of the plant is very pleasing. The flowers are a pale violet or lavender blue, 1–2 cm (0·5–0·75 in) wide with a two-lipped corolla, and are borne in clusters of two to three in the leaf-axils, during April and May. There are several varieties: *albiflorus*, which is white-flowering; *angustifolius* and its form 'Corsican Blue', with rich green foliage and flowers of a bright porcelain blue; and *erectus*, an erect growing form.

Propagate by cuttings, taken with a heel, in August, inserted in sandy soil, under handlights or cold frame. Prune, if desirable, immediately after flowering.

Rubus
Family ROSACEAE

Rubus deliciosus

Among the four hundred species in this group are a few distinctive for their ornamental attractiveness. The stems are prickly, with alternate leaves, lobed and simple, or compounded, flowers five-parted and followed by fruits made up of one-seeded carpels. The hardy species are easily grown in any good garden loam.

Those with simple, lobed leaves include *R. deliciosus*, the Rocky Mountains Bramble, a deciduous shrub of 1·3–2·4 m (5–8 ft), with vine-like leaves, and large, single white flowers in May and June; and *R. odoratus*, North America, 1·8–2·4 m (6–8 ft), handsome with large, vine-like leaves, and panicles of scented, purple flowers, July to September. Then there is a group with stems covered with white waxy coating, showing effectively in winter, such as *R. cockburnianus*, 2·4 m (8 ft), pinnate leaves, purple flowers in June, from China; and *R. thibetanus*, China, 1·8 m (6 ft), with fine pinnate foliage, purple flowers in June. *R. spectabilis*, North America, 1·2–1·8 m (4–6 ft), has trifoliolate leaves, and fragrant, purple-red flowers in April. *R. tricolor*, Korea, makes a good ground cover plant, with heart-shaped leaves.

Propagate by cuttings in August. Prune out shoots immediately after they have fruited.

Ruscus
Family LILIACEAE

Ruscus aculeatus

The genus is one of evergreen sub-shrubs, with green stems, alternate, entire rigid, pointed leathery, deep green leaves, with flowers produced in the centre of the leaves from their mid-ribs, followed by red berries. They will grow almost anywhere in the garden, in any garden soil, and do well in shade.

R. aculeatus is the Butcher's Broom, native to England and the Mediterranean region, making a dwarf-growing shrub, 60–91 cm (2–3 ft), with glossy green leaves, and small white flowers of male or female sex, in March and April. On female plants the flowers give way to red berries, and these make a striking picture. Var *hermaphroditus* is an hermaphrodite form, which berries without the need to plant male and female plants.

R. hypophyllum is a dwarf, to 30 cm (12 in), with unbranched stems, oval leaves, up to 7·5 cm (3 in), with white flowers in small clusters of five or six in the axils of minute bracts on the upper surface of the 'leaves', known to botanists as cladodes. It is native to the Mediterranean, but less hardy than Butcher's Broom.

Propagate by division of the roots in March. No regular pruning is necessary.

Shrubby Sage

Salvia
Family LABIATAE

Salvia chamaedrifolia

The shrubby plants of Sage are few. They are evergreen, with square stems, having opposite, greyish-green leaves, generally round-toothed, and downy with hairs on both sides, and bear two-stamened flowers, somewhat like those of foxgloves, in pairs or whorls in erect terminal racemes. They make attractive bushy shrubs, flowering throughout the summer, and deserve a good, well-drained loam, a sunny position, and, for the more tender species, the shelter of a south or west wall.

The common Sage, *S. officinalis*, of southern Europe, makes a bush of up to 60 cm (2 ft), but is best in its varieties, such as *aurea*, compact form with golden leaves; *icterina*, with green and gold leaves; *purpurascens*, with reddish purple leaves; and *tricolor*, with cream, pink and red variegated leaves. Attractive shrubs are *S. chamaedrifolia*, 30 cm (1 ft) tall, blue flowering, and *S. grahamii*, from Mexico, up to 1·2 m (4 ft), with oval leaves having a black-currant scent, and scarlet tubular flowers from July to autumn, given a sheltered warm spot.

Propagate by cuttings in July or August, under handlights. To keep bushes neat and dense, they may be pinched back occasionally during the growing season.

Santolina
Family COMPOSITAE

Santolina chamaecyparissus

The distinction of this small group of aromatic, evergreen shrubs from the Mediterranean region is in their silvery-white felted shoots and leaves. The leaves are alternate, pinnate or pinnately lobed, and the flowers are daisy-like without ray florets and borne singly but crowded in terminal stalked heads. They are easily grown in any soil that is well drained, and not too rich, and they appreciate full sun.

S. chamaecyparissus, the Lavender Cotton of southern Europe, makes a bushy shrub, and grows to 30–60 cm (1–2 ft), with stems and feathery, pinnately divided lobed leaves silvery-white felted, and yellow buttons of flowers freely borne in attractive masses in long-stalked heads from June to August. Var *corsica* (syn *nana*)is a highly attractive dwarf from 23–30 cm (9–12 in), foliage more intensely white-frosted, and flowers more miniature but just as freely borne. *S. virens* (syn *S. viridis*), southern Europe, grows to 60 cm (2 ft), and has somewhat longer leaves of dark green, and flower-heads of pale yellow on long stalks.

Propagate by cuttings taken with a heel in June or July, inserted in sandy soil, under a handlight. May be trimmed to keep compact and bushy after flowering.

Winter Savory

Satureia
Family LABIATAE

Satureia montana

The genus is one of highly aromatic herbs, but contains one low-growing shrub which may be placed in the shrub garden for its ornamental virtue, while being of usefulness in yielding its leaves for culinary purposes.

S. montana, the Winter Savory, is native to the Mediterranean countries of southern Europe and North Africa; a small semi-evergreen shrub sending up erect stems, 30–37·5 cm (12–15 in) high, with small, linear, entire, opposite leaves, pitted on both sides and with bristly edges. The flowers are small and broad-lipped, and pale purple or whitish, being freely produced in the uppermost leaf-axils in axillary whorls to form dense, but slender, terminal panicles or heads. Its pleasant aromatic character makes this shrub welcome at the front of shrub borders or beds.

Propagate by 'heeled' cuttings taken in June or July, rooted in sandy loam, on a shady border, or under handlights. May also be divided at the roots in March-April. No pruning is necessary.

Senecio
Family COMPOSITAE

Senecio greyii

Of over one thousand two hundred species, this is one of the largest genera, and contains attractively leaved, evergreen shrubs, with foliage consisting of alternate, thickish leaves, silvery or white with felted down, and white or yellow daisy-like flower-heads. They are easily grown, needing only reasonably good, drained, garden loam, and full sun. Their wind-hardiness makes them indispensable for maritime gardens; inland and in the north, warm shelter from searing cold winds is needed.

The hardiest are *S. laxifolius*, New Zealand, growing to 1·2 m (4 ft), with grey downy shoots, lanceolate, blunt-ended leaves, grey-green above, white-felted beneath, and golden-yellow rayed flower-heads in loose, terminal panicles during summer; *S. greyii*, New Zealand, is pleasing but less hardy, growing 1·3 m (5 ft) tall, with stout branchlets and 10·1 cm (4 in) ovate leaves white-felted, and 5 cm (2 in) yellow-rayed flowers in terminal panicles in June and July. *S. reinoldii* (syn *rotundifolius*), of New Zealand, may grow 1·8–6 m (6–20 ft), with almost circular leaves, flowers without ray-florets in June and July, and is excellent against sea winds.

Propagate by cuttings, in a cold frame, in July. Prune after flowering.

Skimmia
Family RUTACEAE

Skimmia japonica var *foremanii*

These small evergreen shrubs are highly attractive for their pleasant green foliage and bright red berries through the winter, and thrive in shade. The leaves are entire and alternate, aromatic when crushed, and the flowers are small and white in closely packed short terminal panicles, unisexual in some species, bisexual in others. They prefer an acid, well-drained soil, enriched with humus.

S. japonica of Japan makes a bush of 0·9–1·3 m (3–5 ft) tall, with ovate leaves, and white, four-parted flowers in small erect panicles, which are unisexual, and only followed by coral-red berries on female plants, interplanted with males. The flowers are scented particularly in var *fragrans*. *S. japonica* var *foremanii*, up to 0·9 m (3 ft), is female, with brilliant red fruits; var *rogersii*, a compact, dwarf female with large red fruits, has an even more dwarf male form, *nana*, free-flowering with small leaves; and var *rubella*, male, has flowers red in the bud during winter. *R. reevesiana* (syn *fortunei*), China, grows to 0·75 cm (30 in), and is hermaphrodite, its white May flowers followed by long-lasting crimson berries.

Propagate by cuttings in July. No regular pruning is needed.

Solanum
Family SOLANACEAE

Solanum crispum

Most of the plants in this genus of over nine hundred species are herbal and of tropical origin, but a few are woody and ornamental in leaf and flower. The leaves are entire and alternate, and the flowers with yellow centres of conspicuous stamens, from the leaf-axils. They will thrive in any good garden loam, in sunlit warm positions and preferably on walls.

The Potato Tree, *S. crispum* of Chile, may be grown as a tall shrub or climber, reaching 3–4·5 m (10–15 ft), with semi-evergreen oval, lanceolate leaves, 12·5 cm (5 in) long, and with large, open corymbs of purple-blue flowers with yellow centres in June and July; its var *autumnale* is even finer with more slender growth, flowers of deeper blue being borne throughout the summer. It should be pruned by being cut hard back each spring. *S. jasminoides*, the Potato Vine of Brazil, is a deciduous twining climber, useful for covering tree-trunks, outhouses, or climbing into tree tops, with lobed leaves, and pale blue flowers in racemes from leaf-axils throughout summer; its var *album* has white flowers. It may be cut to the gound in winter, but with the roots protected, shoots up again.

Propagate by cuttings under glass in July; by seeds sown under glass in February.

Spanish Broom

Spartium
Family LEGUMINOSAE

Spartium junceum

The genus is one of a single species, closely related to *Cytisus* and *Genista*, but distinguished from them botanically in having a one-lipped calyx.

S. junceum is native to the Mediterranean region and the Canary Islands and, as the Spanish Broom, has been grown in this country since the middle of the sixteenth century. Unchecked, it makes a rather straggly, gaunt shrub up to 3 m (10 ft), with long, slender, erect branches and rush-like, green, cylindrical shoots, very sparingly leafed with alternate, linear, small bluish-green leaves or leafless; and bearing large, pea-like shining golden-yellow, fragrant flowers, about 2·5 cm (1 in) long, with wide showy standards, in loose terminal racemes from July into autumn. Var *ochroleucum* is commendable, with flowers of extremely pale yellow. *S. junceum* is most rewarding when it is cut back annually by snipping out shoots after flowering. It grows in most well-drained soils, and is particularly at home on sandy soils, chalky soils and in hot dry places.

Propagate by seeds sown in February under glass, and plant out of pots while juvenile, or by cuttings in a cold frame in July. Prune by cutting previous year's shoots to near their base, March-April.

Spiraea
Family Rosaceae

Spiraea × bumalda

This genus is now wholly one of deciduous shrubs, the herbaceous Spiraeas now being classed elsewhere under *Astilbe*, etc. With alternate leaves, usually toothed or lobed, and small, white, pink or red flowers borne in many-flowered clusters, corymbs or panicles, they are of easy cultivation, being hardy and thriving in free-draining loams, and full sunshine.

One group of species flowers from April to June, bearing white flowers in clusters, racemes or corymbs from branches of the previous year's growth. Noteworthy kinds are: *S.* × *arguta*, a hybrid, known as 'The Bridal Wreath', a shrub of rounded habit, 1·3–2·1 m (5–7 ft) tall, with masses of white flowers in starred clusters, April and May; and *S.* × *vanhouttei*, a hybrid, 1·2–1·8 m (4–6 ft), flowering in June. This group should be pruned right after flowering. A second group flowers June to September, pink to red, or white; and fine examples are: *S.* × *bumalda*, 0·9–1·3 m (3–5 ft), with rosy-red clusters and its var 'Anthony Waterer'; and *S.* × *margaritae*, 1·2–1·3 m (4–5 ft), with rosy-pink flowers in large flat heads.

This group is pruned in winter, by removing flowered shoots. Propagate by cuttings taken in July and August or by offsets in autumn.

Stachyurus
Family STACHYURACEAE

Stachyurus chinensis

In this small genus of deciduous shrubs are two species welcome for their habit of flowering early in February and March. The leaves are alternate, and the small flowers are borne in drooping racemes or spikes, followed by round, berry-like fruits. They are hardy, thriving in free-draining sandy loams or peaty soils, and should be given full sun with shelter from the cold winds from the east and north.

S. chinensis from western China makes a spreading shrub of 1·8–3 m (6–10 ft) tall, with greenish or dark brown branchlets, carrying four parted, small, bell-like, yellow flowers in drooping, stiffish racemes in March, with taper-pointed, ovate, toothed leaves, rounded or cordate at the base, up to 12·5 cm (5 in) long, and forming small, red-cheeked, greenish-yellow berries by autumn. *S. praecox* is a Japanese species of similar habit, growing 1·8–3 m (6–10 ft), with reddish-brown shoots which are smooth and shining, and pale yellow flowers in drooping sprays, 5–10 cm (2–4 in) long, a week or two before those of *S. chinensis*; the leaves are more lance-shaped, and the fruits greenish-yellow and a trifle larger.

Propagate by 'heeled' cuttings under glass in July; by seeds in spring. No regular pruning is required.

Staphylea
Family STAPHYLEACEAE

Staphylea colchica

The plants of this genus make deciduous shrubs, tall-growing, with opposite, toothed, trifoliolate, sometimes pinnate, leaves, panicles of small translucent white flowers in spring, followed by conspicuous, inflated, bladder-like seed-capsules, responsible for their common name. They are hardy, and thrive in soil rich in organic matter and well drained, and in sunny positions.

The most popular species is *S. colchica* from the Caucasus, grown as a shrub to 3 m (10 ft) tall, with leaves of three or five finely toothed, ovate leaflets, glossy green beneath, arranged pinnately, erect sprays of pure small white flowers, scented as the tuberose, in May, and bladder-like fruits later. Its var *coulombieri* is similar, but with longer leaves, and more compact clusters of white flowers in May, and bladder-like fruits later, and altogether of more graceful habit. *S. pinnata*, St. Anthony's Nut, of south Europe, grows to 3·7 m (12 ft high), with dull green pinnate leaves, and flowers in terminal, drooping panicles. *S.* × *elegans* (*S. colchica* × *S. pinnata*) is a hybrid of quality, and has a form *hessei* of which the white flowers are flushed reddish purple.

Propagate by cuttings in July or August or by ripe seeds sown in autumn. No regular pruning is needed.

Stephanandra
Family ROSACEAE

Stephanandra tanakae

The deciduous shrubs forming this group of plants are of pleasing, elegant and graceful habit, with alternate, trilobed leaves, sharply toothed and long-pointed, and bearing small, greenish or yellowish white, five-petalled, star-like flowers in terminal panicles up to 10 cm (4 in) long. They are perfectly hardy, and do well in any well-drained garden loam, in sunshine or light shade.

Only two species are in cultivation. *S. incisa* of China and Japan becomes a shrub 1·8–2·4 m (6–8 ft) tall, of dense, rounded habit, with zigzag, wiry shoots, with roughly triangular leaves, deeply-lobed and fern-like, and greenish-white flowers, crowded in feathery, terminal sprays in June. In autumn, the foliage colours pleasingly. The Japanese *S. tanakae* makes a shrub of 1·3–1·8 m (5–6 ft), with slender, arching, bright brown stems, and twiggy branchlets, clothed with bright green, triangular, double-toothed, sharply pointed leaves, up to 12·5 cm (5 in) long, and bearing white flowers in somewhat loose terminal panicles in June. In autumn, the foliage colours yellow and orange.

Propagate by cuttings in August; by division in March. Prune by cutting old growth back in winter or in March.

Stranvaesia
Family ROSACEAE

Stranvaesia davidiana

The most attractive quality of the evergreen shrubs of this genus is their well-displayed, large clusters of scarlet, haw-like berries, against alternate, leathery, lanceolate leaves, up to 10 cm (4 in) in length. The flowers are white, and are borne in large, terminal, branched clusters in June. They thrive in peaty or acid loam soils, and are best placed in well-sunned positions.

S. davidiana, China, is a hardy vigorous shrub, up to 6·1 m (20 ft) tall or more, with entire, dark green, oval, leathery leaves, white flowers in three-inch clustered heads in June, giving way to trusses of bright scarlet berries in autumn. Its var *salicifolia* of west China, is similar but makes more upright growth to 6·1 m (20 ft), and has narrow, oblong, pointed leaves, with 7·5 cm (3 in) panicles of white flowers in June, followed by round red berries in drooping clusters; and another var, *undulata*, is a spreading dome-shaped shrub, growing to 2·4 m (8 ft) tall, with white, red anthered flowers, in clusters, in June, followed by orange-crimson berries in the autumn; *Fructu-luteo*, a form of *S. davidiana* var *undulata*, bears yellow fruits.

Propagate by seeds, sown under glass in February. No regular pruning is needed.

Styrax
Family STYRACACEAE

Styrax japonica

This genus is one of about one hundred species, but only the deciduous small trees or shrubs are hardy enough for Britain. They make delightful specimens, with alternate, ovate, short-stalked leaves, and white bell-shaped flowers, 2·5 cm (1 in) across, in racemes or clusters borne freely at the ends of short side twigs in June, followed by small egg-shaped fruits in a persistent calyx. They are well suited to the open garden in the south and west, but otherwise need a sunny protected wall. An acid loam or rich peat or leafmould soil suits them well.

The hardiest species are the Japanese *S. japonica*, making a beautiful large shrub of 3–6·1 m (10–20 ft) tall, with horizontal spreading branches, lit with hanging, pure white, five-lobed flowers, like open snowdrops, on slender stalks in rows, amid oval dark shining green leaves; *S. hemsleyana* of China, which grows more tree-like to 9 m (28 ft), with orbicular leaves, up to 15 cm (6 in) long, and racemes of twenty to thirty white flowers, up to 15 cm (6 in) long; and *S. obassia*, Japan, large shrub or tree to 9 m (28 ft), with the largest orbicular leaves of 15–20 cm (6–8 in) long, and fragrant white flowers in terminal racemes, up to 18 cm (7 in) long.

Propagate by cuttings or layering in July or August.

Symphoricarpos
Family CAPRIFOLIACEAE

Symphoricarpos albus

This group of small, hardy deciduous shrubs is chiefly valued for the attractive berrying. The leaves grow opposite, short-stalked, entire or lobed, and the flowers are small, pink or white, in axillary or terminal clusters. The shrubs are completely hardy, but have little beauty of habit, and are useful for growing in shade where little else will grow, in the wild garden, or in coverts, needing only the most ordinary soil.

S. rivularis (syn *albus laevigatus*), the Snowberry of North America, makes a thicket of erect stems, with small, almost circular, or irregularly lobed leaves, small pink to white, bell-shaped flowers in short terminal racemes in June to August, giving way to white, berry-like fruits, to 1·8 m (6 ft) high, 13 mm (0·5 in) wide. *S. albus*, eastern North America, is similar, but grows only to 1·2 m (4 ft), with pink flowers in axillary clusters in July to August, followed by white berries. The hybrids *S.* × *doorenbosii* 'Magic Berry', pink berries, and 'Mother of Pearl', white, flushed pink, are good small, compact plants.

Propagate by detaching suckers in March; by cuttings in July; by seeds. No regular pruning is required.

Lilac

Syringa
Family OLEACEAE

Syringa reflexa

The Lilacs form a group of deciduous shrubs of notable flowering beauty, having opposite leaves, and small, four-lobed flowers, generally scented, and freely borne in terminal or axillary panicles. They are hardy, and are easily grown in most soils, doing particularly well on chalk, and in sunny positions.

S. vulgaris, east Europe, is the Common Lilac, up to 6·1 m (20 ft), bearing panicles of scented lilac bloom in terminal pairs in May, and having many forms of which 'Clarke's Giant', lilac-blue, 'Maud Notcutt', white, 'Massena', purple-red, 'Primrose', and 'Souvenir de Louis Späth', purple, are fine singles; and 'Charles Joly', dark-red, 'Madame Lemoine', white, and 'Mrs E. Harding', red, are good doubles. Outstanding species are *S. emodi*, Himalaya, 2·4–3·7 m (8–12 ft) tall, long, oval leaves, whitish beneath, white or mauve flowers; the Persian Lilac, *S.* × *persica*, neat and bushy to 1·8 m (6 ft), with highly scented lilac flowers; and *S. reflexa*, 1·8–3·7 m (6–12 ft) with arching panicles of deep pink bloom; while *S.* × *chinensis*, the Rouen Lilac, is a highly scented hybrid, with several vars, and *S.* × *josiflexa* 'Bellicent', pink and 'Desdemona', reddish-purple, are fine Canadian hybrids.

Propagate species by heeled cuttings in July or August. Others are grafted.

Tamarix
Family TAMARICACEAE

Tamarix pentandra

The shrubs of this genus are naturally found in maritime areas, and have slender branches lined with alternate, tiny scale-like leaves which give them the appearance of green plumes; the flowers are very small, pink or white and closely packed in straight cylindrical racemes, often making up large terminal panicles. These shrubs are excellent wind-resisters, for seaside gardens, though they will also grow inland, preferably in good, moist loamy soil, and in full sun.

T. tetrandra comes from the Mediterranean region, a deciduous shrub, growing 3–4·5 m (10–15 ft) high, with tiny, bright pink flowers in straight spikes from shoots of the previous year in May. *T. gallica*, the French Tamarisk, an evergreen shrub of 1·2–3 m (4–10 ft), with purplish branchlets, and short, slender racemes of pink; and *T. pentandra* (syn *T. pallasii*), south-east Europe, growing 3–3·7 m (10–12 ft), with tiny deciduous leaves, and rosy-pink flowers in racemes making feathery panicles; with a var *rubra*, having rosy-red bloom.

Propagate by cuttings taken with a heel, July or August. Prune October to March as needed.

Shrubby Germander

Teucrium
Family LABIATAE

Teucrium fruticans

The genus is better known for its plants of medical value. A few shrub species may, however, be used with distinctive effect in sheltered gardens of the mild south-west; their square stems, beset with opposite leaves, and purple or rose flowers being characteristic. They like well-drained, open, loamy soil, and warm sheltered situations in the sun.

The Shrubby Germander of southern Europe, *T. fruticans*, makes a bushy shrub of 0·6–1·2 m (2–4 ft), with white-felted, forking stems, entire, ovate, evergreen leaves, to 4 cm (1·5 in) long, and Salvia-like lavender-blue flowers in erect, leafy racemes from June into October, and is one of the most effective silvery-leaved shrubs in its season. It has a var *azureum*, collected in the Atlas Mountains, with more slender growth, flowers of a deeper blue and more tender. *T. marum* is the Cat Thyme, a dwarf shrub of 30 cm (12 in) or less, with small, hairy green leaves, white-felted beneath, and rose-coloured flowers, from the Mediterranean region. It is hardy, but attractive to cats and they roll on it.

Propagate by cuttings taken in July or August, under handlights or in a frame. No pruning is needed.

Ulex
Family LEGUMINOSAE

Ulex minor

The evergreen shrubs of this group with their spiny stems, and yellow pea-like flowers, are familiar to every country lover. Leaves are absent except on seedlings, where they are trifoliolate and alternate. They are useful grouped to give masses of colour, and to induce free flowering, are best planted in poor, dry or shallow soils, and thrive on broken limestone or chalk, given full sun.

U. europaeus is the Furze, Gorse, or Whin native to the countryside of Britain and western Europe, growing 0·6–1·8 m (2–6 ft) tall, with dense spiny stems, and grooved spines, and bearing its golden-yellow, pea-like flowers freely from March to June, followed by 13 mm (0·5 in) long, hairy pods. The double-flowering var *plenus*, in which the stamens of the flower have become petals, is even more colourful. The Petty Whin or Dwarf Gorse, *U. minor*, found wild in Britain and western Europe, makes a small dense shrub of 30–60 cm (12–24 in) high, with its golden-yellow flowers crowding short, upright, spiny stems from July to October, effective in association with *Calluna, Erica* or *Caryopteris*.

Propagate by cuttings in July or August, under a handlight or a frame, or by seeds, sown in pots, and transplanted young. Prune immediately after flowering.

Vaccinium
Family ERICACEAE

Vaccinium corymbosum

The Vacciniums are a group of deciduous and evergreen shrubs with alternate, short-stalked leaves, small, white or pink, bell-shaped flowers, in axillary or terminal racemes, and fruit berries which are often useful for pies, sauces and preserves. They need moist, peaty and lime-free soil, and succeed in sun or shade.

Of the deciduous species, hardy pleasing kinds are *V. arctostaphylos*, the Caucasian Whortleberry, of 2·4–3 m (8–10 ft), with ovate leaves, colouring red in autumn, axillary clusters of whitish flowers in June, then purple berries; *V. corymbosum*, North America, a branching shrub to 2·4 m (8 ft), has ovate leaves, pinkish May flowers, and blue berries, and fine autumn colouring, and *V. myrtillus*, the native Bilberry, for good low ground cover. Good evergreens include *V. bracteatum*, China, 0·9–1·3 m (3–5 ft) tall, scented, bracted, white egg-shaped flowers, July and August, and red berries; *V. ovatum*, North America, upright to 2·4 m (8 ft), with red stems, pinkish-white May flowers, black berries; and *V. vitis-idaea*, a charming creeper, 15–30 cm (6–12 in), with pink flowers and dark-red, edible fruits.

Propagate by cuttings in July or August; by layering in autumn; by seeds in spring.

Viburnum
Family CAPRIFOLIACEAE

Viburnum farreri (syn *fragrans*)

Some most beautiful ornamental shrubs are in this genus. The leaves are opposite and simple, the flowers small in branched clusters, often fragrant, and followed by coloured berries. They are easily grown in all but poor, dry soils, and only a short list is attempted here.

Deciduous, the Chinese *V. farreri* (syn *V. fragrans*), 1·3–3 m (5–10 ft), is indispensable for its highly-scented white to pink flowers in winter; *V.* × *bodnantense* 'Dawn' is a hybrid with larger flowers; *V. carlesii*, Korea, 1·2–2·4 m (4–8 ft), is white-flowering and fragrant in April and May; *V. betulifolium*, China, grows to 3 m (10 ft), flowering white in June, and red berries in autumn; *V. opulus sterile*, Europe, the Snowball Tree, grows to 3·7 m (12 ft), with balls of white June flowers; *V. plicatum* var *tomentosum*, China, to 3 m (10 ft), has flat clusters of white June flowers, larger in v. *mariesii*. Of the evergreens, *V. davidii*, China, to 1·3 m (5 ft), June flowering, handsome fruiting; *V.* × *burkwoodii*, hybrid, 1·2–1·8 m (4–6 ft), fragrant pinkish-white flowers in April; and *V. tinus*, the Laurustinus, south Europe, and var 'Eve Price', bloom December to April.

Propagate by cuttings taken in July or August; by seeds. No regular pruning is needed.

Weigela
Family CAPRIFOLIACEAE

Weigela florida var *variegata*

Formerly listed under *Diervilla*, this is a group of deciduous shrubs, growing to 1·8–2·4 m (6–8 ft) tall, with opposite, ovate, long-pointed, evenly toothed, and short-stalked leaves, and five-parted, funnel-shaped flowers, resembling those of Foxglove, from the uppermost leaf-axils in clusters, in spring. The plants are hardy, and will grow best in good, moist loams, limy or not, with some protection against damaging late frosts.

Of the species, *W. florida*, China, with arching stems, and flowers in deep pink outside, white within, in clusters of three or four in May and June; var *variegata*, yellow-edged leaves; *W. middendorffiana*, 0·6–1·2 m (2–4 ft), with terminal clusters of sulphur-yellow flowers in April and May; *W. praecox*, Korea, to 1·8 m (6 ft), with long, rose, yellow-throated flowers in April; *W. venusta*, Korea, to 1·8 m (6 ft), with rose-pink flowers in May; and the hybrids, 'Abel Carrière', large pink flowers; 'Bouquet Rose', silver-pink; 'Conquête', rose-pink; 'Eva Rathke', deep crimson; 'Mont Blanc', white; 'Newport Red', rich red; and 'Styriaca', crimson, are rewarding.

Propagate by cuttings of young shoots, May–June; of firm mature shoots in August–October. Prune immediately after flowering.

Wisteria
Family Leguminosae

Wisteria sinensis

This genus is one of the most beautiful, deciduous, twining climbing shrubs, with long, unequally pinnate, alternate leaves, and lone, drooping racemes of blue to white flowers, freely produced. They are hardy, and thrive in good loamy soils, even on chalk, and do best in full sun, trained on walls, pergolas, or old trees.

The finest of the species is undoubtedly *W. sinensis* of China, capable of reaching 30 m (98 ft) in time, have nine- to thirteen-leafleted pinnate leaves, and sweetly scented, lilac mauve flowers in racemes 23–30 cm (9–12 in) long, in May and June. *W. venusta*, Japan, grows to 9 m (30 ft), with downy pinnate leaves, and racemes of white flowers, 10–15 cm (4–6 in) long, in May and June; and has a double-flowering var *plena*. *W. floribunda* of Japan, growing 9–12 m (30–40 ft), with thirteen- to nineteen-foliolate, pinnate leaves of dark glossy green, and racemes of scented, violet-blue flowers, up to 25 cm (10 in) long; and *macrobotrys* (syn *S. multijuga*) has racemes 0·6–1 m (2–3 ft) long.

Propagate by layering in May. Prune lateral leafy shoots by half in late July, and again to two buds in late winter.

Yucca
Family LILIACEAE

Yucca filamentosa

This group of American evergreen shrubs and trees, known picturesquely as 'Candles of the Lord', are suited to specimen, courtyard or formal planting. Their leaves are linear, long, narrow and spine-tipped, crowded radially in tufts; and the flowers are large, bell-shaped, usually a shade of white, large, drooping or erect panicles or racemes. The hardy species require well-drained soil, appreciating hot sandy loams, and the sunniest positions.

The best species for most gardens is *Y. recurvifolia*, a native of south-east USA, with naked stem up to 1·8 m (6 ft), spine-tipped leaves, up to 90 cm (3 ft) long, arching back, and creamy-white, 5 cm (2 in) flowers in an erect panicle, 0·9–1·2 m (3–4 ft) high, in August and September. *Y. filamentosa*, south-east USA, is stemless, with stiff leaves, 50–75 cm (20–30 in) long, having marginal curly threads, with a panicle of creamy-white flowers up to 1·8 m (6 ft) high, in July and August. *Y. gloriosa*, Adam's Needle, has a short stem, with leaves up to 60 cm (2 ft) long, 7·5 cm (3 in) wide, and creamy-white flowers in an erect panicle 0·9–1·2 m (3–4 ft) high, July to September.

Propagate by root cuttings of 7·5 cm (3 in) in March, in a propagating frame; by offset shoots, or division, in March–April; by seeds in October.

Zenobia
Family Ericaceae

Zenobia pulverulenta

The distinctive shrubs of this genus are deciduous, with alternate, ovate, blunt-tipped, and distantly toothed leaves, and white, bell-shaped, small flowers drooping at the ends of long stalks in axillary clusters in June and July. They are hardy, need a lime-free, well-drained soil, and do best in partial shade.

Z. pulverulenta (syns *Z. speciosa* var *pulverulenta*; *Andromeda pulverulenta*, *A. dealbata*) is native to the south-east USA, and makes a charming shrub growing 0·9 m (3 ft) tall, with its young shoots and ovalish leaves covered with a bluish-white or glaucous bloom, and bearing flowers like those of Lily-of-the-Valley, 13 mm (0·5 in) across, in stalked clusters during late June and early July. *Z. speciosa* (syns *Z. pulverulenta* var *nuda*; *Andromeda cassinifolia*) is equally beautiful, but differs in the leaves and shoots being green without bloom and the flowers slightly smaller.

Propagate by layers in May; by cuttings in July, August; or by seeds sown in cold frame in October. Prune after flowering, removing spent flowering ends of branches, and some of the oldest wood occasionally.

Index

Classifications in this index follow the style used throughout the book. Thus, a family name is printed in capitals and small capitals (eg, ARALIACEAE), the generic name in italics (eg, *Aronia*), and a popular or common name in roman type (eg, Adam's Needle).